Physical Resources Foundation Report
White Sands National Monument

Natural Resource Report NPS/NRPC/NRR —2009/166

Jeffery Bennett
Big Bend National Park
P.O. Box 129
Big Bend National Park, TX, 79830
(prepared water resources sections in report)

Douglas Wilder
NPS Midwest Region Geospatial Support Center
120 Russell Labs
163C Linden Drive
Madison, WI 53706
(prepared geologic resources sections in report)

November 2009

U.S. Department of the Interior
National Park Service
Natural Resource Program Center
Fort Collins, Colorado

The National Park Service, Natural Resource Program Center publishes a range of reports that address natural resource topics of interest and applicability to a broad audience in the National Park Service and others in natural resource management, including scientists, conservation and environmental constituencies, and the public.

The Natural Resource Report Series is used to disseminate high-priority, current natural resource management information with managerial application. The series targets a general, diverse audience, and may contain NPS policy considerations or address sensitive issues of management applicability.

All manuscripts in the series receive the appropriate level of peer review to ensure that the information is scientifically credible, technically accurate, appropriately written for the intended audience, and designed and published in a professional manner. This report received formal peer review by subject-matter experts who were not directly involved in the collection, analysis, or reporting of the data, and whose background and expertise put them on par technically and scientifically with the authors of the information.

Views, statements, findings, conclusions, recommendations, and data in this report are those of the author(s) and do not necessarily reflect views and policies of the National Park Service, U.S. Department of the Interior. Mention of trade names or commercial products does not constitute endorsement or recommendation for use by the National Park Service.

This report is available from the Natural Resource Publications Management website http://www.nature.nps.gov/publications/NRPM

Please cite this publication as:

Bennett, J., and D. Wilder. 2009. Physical resources foundation report, White Sands National Monument. Natural Resource Report NPS/NRPC/NRR—2009/166. National Park Service, Fort Collins, Colorado.

NPS 142/100371, November 2009

Contents

Appendices

Figures

Tables

Executive Summary

In accordance with the NPS 2004 Park Planning Program Standards, parks are to prepare a *Foundation for Park Planning and Management* document (Foundation Document), which describes its purpose, significance, primary interpretive themes and special mandates, identifying and analyzing those resources and values determined to warrant primary consideration (*Fundamental* and *Important Resources and Values*) in park planning and management. The *Foundation Document* may be developed as the first phase of a park's general management planning process or independently of the *General Management Plan*.

This *Physical Resources Foundation Report* is designed to support development of the *Foundation Document* for White Sands National Monument (WHSA) and to be used as a reference for the *General Management Plan*, as needed.

The primary objectives of this report are to:

1. Build upon the monument's purpose and significance statements and identify the *fundamental* physical resources critical to achieving WHSA's purpose and maintaining its significance.
2. Provide background information for WHSA's *fundamental* physical resources (current condition, related trends, and issues/threats).
3. Define the relevant laws and policies that support management decisions for the priority physical resources and identify stakeholder interest.

White Sands National Monument Legislation, Purpose and Significance Statements

The 1933 Presidential Proclamation (No. 2025, 47 Stat. 2551) creating White Sands National Monument states:

"Whereas it appears that the public interest would be promoted by including the lands hereinafter described within a national monument for the preservation of the white sands and additional features of scenic, scientific, and educational interest..."

From this proclamation, the following Purpose Statement, which describes the specific reasons for establishing the national monument, was generated for WHSA (from the White Sands National Monument Strategic Plan, FY2001-2005):

"...the purpose of White Sands National Monument is:
- *preserve a portion of the world's largest gypsum dunefield and additional features of scenic, scientific, and education interest; and*
- *provide for educational and recreational opportunities compatible with the protection of those resources for future generations."*

The WHSA Significance Statement that defines what is most important about the national monument's physical resources and values is:

"The primary significance of White Sands National Monument lies in its superlative geologic values. The dunefield is actively migrating. Dune movement is an easily observed example of a dynamic process. The story of gypsum sand, its formation into dunes and their movement, as well as the stories of the larger geological events, can be learned at White Sands, the world's largest gypsum dune field."

Foundation Document

Building from the WHSA Purpose and Significance statements, it is recommended that geologic and water resources be defined as "fundamental resources" at WHSA, warranting the highest level of preservation. For a NPS *Foundation Document*, the following questions are asked about the park-specific priority resources and values:

1. What is the importance of the geologic and water resources?

The WHSA was established by Congress to preserve a portion of the largest gypsum dune field in the world and additional features of scenic, scientific, and educational interest. These unique geologic features are ultimately tied to both the historic and current geologic and hydrologic processes of the Tularosa Basin. Some of the specific justifications for the "fundamental resource" recommendation are listed below:

Geologic Resources

- WHSA preserves 115 square miles of the world's largest gypsum dune field (275 square miles). Many of the area's organisms have rapidly adapted to the white sands by modifying color to match the sands, becoming distinct species and subspecies. The white sands are the driver of the local ecosystem and the species within it.

- WHSA has been identified as a premier U.S. site for yardangs (an elongated wind-abraded ridge found in desert environments).

- Plant and crystal pedestals are an important subject of research. The formation mechanism of pedestals is not well understood.

- Bajadas on the western side of the monument distribute water, have distinct plant communities and soil types, and are the recharge area for water to the basin.

- Fossilized mammoth tracks and other paleontological resources within the monument are indicators of past climate and may provide information on the climatic conditions during the Pleistocene.

- The biological soil crusts at WHSA are communities of cyanobacteria and fungus that occupy an intermediate ecological position between active dunes and heavily vegetated surfaces. Soil crusts are indicators of ecosystem stability, health, and climate change.

- Lake Otero sediments represent the most recent lake history and hold clues to dune processes, habitat for early humans, and regional geologic history. These sediments may also include a record of micrometeorite falls that may have affected mammoth and bison populations in the area.

- White Sands is recognized as an analog for Mars and the Moon. Gypsum dunes, crystals pedestals and other formations are known to occur both at White Sands and on Mars. Research in the monument may reveal significant information about physical processes and conditions on Mars and the Moon.

Water Resources

- The occurrence of a shallow aquifer within WHSA is of critical importance (Barud-Zubillaga, 2000). Groundwater is a major factor in controlling dune stability and movement. Saturated sediments are more resistant of the erosive forces of wind.

- Groundwater quality in the monument is naturally poor for consumption but important for dune stability. Saline groundwater precipitates minerals within the wind blown sand which cement the soft gypsum grains together.

- In the context of the ecosystem of WHSA, the unsaturated zone is very important to dune stability. Infiltrating precipitation and surface waters, along with groundwater provided by capillary action, are important for plants, burrowing animals, and soil function.

- Groundwater is important to the hydrologic processes of Lake Lucero. Fluctuating groundwater levels and the influx of surface water dissolve and re-precipitate (cycle) gypsum, continually reworking the lake bed. Selenite pedestals are a unique feature of Lake Lucero.

- Based on reported visitor activity, Lake Lucero is an important natural feature of popular interest to the public.

2. What is the adequacy of the existing geologic and water resources information?

Geologic Resources

Existing Information:

- Numerous studies have been conducted to both inventory geologic resources and better understand dune processes. Early geologic reconnaissance work was done by Herrick (1904).

- KellerLynn (2008) provides a thorough summary of geologic resources identified during project scoping for the NPS Geologic Resources Inventory program.

- There are reports and ongoing research to ground truth remote sensing data. This work proposed age dates and a time line for the growth of the dune field (Szybkiewicz et al., 2008).

- A generalized summary of the paleontological resources in the monument was prepared in 2007 (National Park Service, 2007).

- A comprehensive summary of White Sands' local geology was completed in 2002 (New Mexico Geological Society, 2002).

Needed Data/Information:

- Bibliography of dune research, including a catalog of existing data and imagery should be compiled and loaded into the NPS NatureBib database.

- It is not clear whether the dune field is growing or shrinking. Origin and timing of dune formation, dune dynamics, and the interactions between deflation of the dunes and playa lakes are not well understood and are current subjects of research. Additional research in these subjects is important to better frame monument management decisions.

- A thorough inventory of the paleontological resources in the monument is needed. The inventory should include the location, stratigraphic position, and age of all paleontological resources, including fossil mammoth tracks and microfossils in the lake bed sediments.

- A more detailed soils map is needed to better match the scale at which monument management decisions and activities occur.

- Additional information is needed on soil crust resilience, recovery rates and areal extents of different biological soil crusts occurring in the monument.

- An inventory of yardang locations and conditions is needed to plan for the protection of this unique resource.

- The mechanism of crystal pedestal formation is unknown and the subject of current research.

Water Resources

Existing Information:

- Available information on water resources within the Tularosa Basin consists of water resource and hydrogeologic reports dating back to the beginning of the twentieth century, and geologic data gathered in support of the water resource reports. The scarcity of water within the basin prompted significant investigation on the nature and occurrence of water as early as 1915 (Meinzer and Hare).

- The NPS Chihuahuan Desert Inventory and Monitoring Network has produced several reports for park units within the network, including WHSA, that contain historic water resources data.

- The NPS Water Resources Division completed a comprehensive summary of existing surface water quality data for WHSA (National Park Service, 1997).

- Information on the occurrence and persistence of contaminants from the Department of Defense (DOD) activities is available from USGS and DOD reports (KellerLynn, 2003).

- An inventory of wetlands on neighboring DOD property was completed in 2004 (Martin et al., 2004).

Needed Data/Information:

- Groundwater flow models have been produced for the purposes of regional planning (Huff, 2004). Available models are not scaled properly to incorporate and evaluate potential threats posed by water resource development. A single basin wide groundwater flow model that incorporates all users is needed.

- The relationship between groundwater dynamics, the Jarilla Fault, and the ecology and stability of the dunes has not been fully investigated. Information on recharge to the shallow aquifer within the dunefield is inadequate.

- Monitoring wells within WHSA provide opportunities for shallow monitoring of groundwater resources, but are not oriented in the most effective way to capture potential groundwater contaminant plumes from Holloman Air Force Base (HAFB).

- The relationship between groundwater elevations, precipitation, and flows within the Lost River is not understood.

- Surface water features like the Lost River are not systematically monitored for contaminants.

3. What are the current states or conditions and the related trends of the geologic and water resources?

Geologic Resources

- The condition of the eolian system appears very sensitive to changes in groundwater elevations (Fryberger, 2001).

- It is not clear whether or not fossil mammoth tracks, lake sediment micro fossils and yardangs are eroding or not. However, Fryberger (2001) has stated the need for more research on yardangs, noting that these features are presently undamaged.

- Biologic soil crusts appear robust; however, potential problems are unknown. Crusts in sulfate-rich soils form quickly (within a few years) so that foot-traffic disturbances are less likely to create long-term problems.

Water Resources

Water Quantity

- Twice as much precipitation falls on the higher Sacramento Mountains as does on the San Andres Mountains on the western side of the basin. Hence, water extraction is concentrated on the eastern side of the basin.

- The New Mexico State Engineer's Office, on May 19, 1997, recognized the Tularosa Basin as a mined basin (for groundwater resources) and instituted policies and procedures to allow a specified amount of de-watering during a forty-year planning period. The office specified that water level decline rates should not exceed 2.5 feet per year. Water conservation strategies such as reuse of gray water and innovative technologies like the desalinization facility advanced by the City of Alamogordo, other communities, and federal agencies have and will help slow the decline in groundwater levels.

- Groundwater that supports the hydrologic function of the playa and dune system is supplied by a regional groundwater gradient that transmits water from the surrounding mountains to the playas at the basin center. The process is complicated by the presence of the north-south trending Jarilla Fault located along the eastern boundary of WHSA. The eastern side of the fault has moved upward relative to the western block and has brought bedrock to or very near the surface, effectively separating the two sides of the basin fill aquifer. From where the fault intersects the surface the geologic formations dip to the east. Groundwater moving from the Sacramento Mountains westward into the basin is brought to the surface by these rising beds where it discharges as springs and wetlands primarily on DOD property to the east of WHSA. Climate forces place heavy evaporation pressure on these resources. Some current groundwater flow models assume all this water evaporates and therefore presumes these resources would not contribute to water resources in the western basin. However, groundwater from the eastern side of the basin may not all evaporate and may contribute to recharge of groundwater resources in the western side. Groundwater from the eastern sub-basin may play a role in maintaining groundwater levels in the western sub-basin.

- Within the last 60 years, four springs have dried up within the monument including Garton Pond, adobe wells (a hand dug well), and a spring that was shown on a 1960 topographic map.

Water Quality

- The water quality in WHSA is heavily impacted by the high evaporation rate of the region. Local ground and surface water naturally violate drinking water and aquatic use standards for chloride and sulfate.

- Fresh water is limited in the basin and occurs in alluvial fans on the basin margins and in gravel layers that transmit groundwater without contact with gypsiferous sediments. Fresh water to supply park functions must come from outside the park. Water is delivered by pipeline from the Boles Well field south of Alamogordo in the summer and from HAFB, which draws the water from Bonito Lake in the winter.

- Information on the occurrence and persistence of contaminants from Department of Defense activities state that no current water quality problems have been identified in WHSA (KellerLynn, 2003).

4. What are the current and potential threats to geologic and water resources?

Geologic Resources

- Saltcedar (*Tamarisk sp.*) creates vegetative pedestals by drying out the surrounding sand, which erodes away, altering dune distribution. Resulting pedestals change local wind patterns imposing further control on where dunes form. Continued influence of saltcedar may result in distribution patterns of dunes reflecting occurrence of the invasive species.

- Certain man-made structures may concentrate the effects of erosion and threaten both natural and monument facility resources. Road culverts on the west side of the monument have accelerated erosion and caused damage to some cultural resources, specifically the Huntington Site. Additional man-made structures affecting erosion include buried fiber optic cables, water lines, roads, and trails.

- Dissolution around buried features such as water lines and fiber optic cables may cause the formation of sink holes and other karst-like features. Parking lots and buildings are also at risk as rainwater runoff and water from other sources dissolves underlying gypsum layers.

- Erosion or deposition of sand due to wind affects WHSA facility development. Maintenance decisions for the location of new facilities should consider wind erosion patterns across the monument.

- Debris flows sourced on the west side of the monument can transport large boulders onto roads and destroy fences. There are also documented cases of fatalities due to debris flows on the missile range and in a nearby BLM campground.

Water Resources

- The City of El Paso, Texas, extracts groundwater from the Tularosa-Hueco Bolson and recently constructed a desalinization facility to allow for increased utilization of the aquifer. Reporting by the El Paso Water Utilities indicates that water level declines due to pumping will propagate to the north across the state line and into the vicinity of WHSA (El Paso Water Utilities, 2004).

- Declines in groundwater elevations are expected within the Tularosa Basin and present a significant and impending threat to WHSA's dunefield. It is unclear how water level declines will impact the shallow aquifer within WHSA. However, this uncertainty should not dissuade management from monitoring every water permit application to the State Engineer's Office.

- The limited nature of freshwater within the basin makes the supply vulnerable to over production and pollution. Over production could concentrate brines, locally alter the direction of flow of groundwater and impact the water quality as well as the quantity of perennial fresh water sources like the Lost River

- The use of hazardous materials on White Sands Missile Range (WSMR) represents a potential threat to WHSA's natural resources and visitor safety. A groundwater monitoring system is in place and to date no contamination has been found. However, hazardous waste sites and groundwater contaminants have been identified on WSMR. With increasing demands on groundwater resources in the region, changes in groundwater flow could enhance off-site migration of contaminants.

- Saltcedars (*Tamarisk sp.*) have invaded arroyos, springs and areas with a shallow water table. Saltcedar encroachment has apparently lowered water tables in portions of the park and increased dune mobility. Saltcedars can also degrade water quality.

Climate Change

Climate change may have a dramatic impact on WHSA. Both the ecological and physical systems currently active in the monument are at risk with large permanent changes in regional precipitation, wind averages, and temperature.

- Changes in temperature and precipitation regimes in the surrounding mountains may shorten the run-off season and change aquifer recharge patterns.

- Warmer, drier conditions could result in larger deflation areas within the dunefield; reactivation of dunes could occur with potentially larger dunes forming; less runoff available to feed Lake Lucero would create more dunes moving out of the lake beds. Changing precipitation cycles could impact biological crusts on soils.

- Warmer, drier conditions will alter water supply patterns and likely increase the reliance on groundwater as a primary source of domestic, industrial and agricultural water. A drop in the water table could impact dune formation and retention.

- Changing atmospheric conditions, including an increase in carbon dioxide will alter vegetation patterns and communities. Dune stabilizing vegetation could decrease. Shifting range conditions in uplands could alter aquifer recharge patterns.

Experience with complex ecosystem dynamics strongly suggests that stressors that drive ecosystems in any direction away from the natural range of variability of conditions under which they developed will have adverse impacts on that system. Ecohydrologic systems such as WHSA can be highly sensitive to hydroclimatic factors, particularly water quantity, water quality, the probability of extreme events, and flow volumes, rates, and timing. Determining the impacts on WHSA will require additional region-specific, and ecosystem-specific, research.

Two additional questions presented in a typical park *Foundation Document* are:

5. **Which laws and policies apply to the geologic and water resources, and what guidance do they provide?**

6. **Who are the stakeholders who have an interest in WHSA's geologic and water resources?**

These last two questions are answered in the main body of this report.

Introduction

White Sands National Monument (WHSA) was established by Presidential Proclamation in 1933 for "… *the preservation of the white sands and additional features of scenic, scientific, and educational interest…*". From this proclamation, the following Purpose Statement, which describes the specific reasons for establishing the national monument, was generated for WHSA (from the White Sands National Monument Strategic Plan, FY2001-2005):

> "…*the purpose of White Sands National Monument is:*
> - *preserve a portion of the world's largest gypsum dunefield and additional features of scenic, scientific, and education interest; and*
> - *provide for educational and recreational opportunities compatible with the protection of those resources for future generations.*"

Building from the Purpose Statement, the WHSA Significance Statement that defines what is most important about the national monument's physical resources and values is:

> "*The primary significance of White Sands National Monument lies in its superlative geologic values. The dunefield is actively migrating. Dune movement is an easily observed example of a dynamic process. The story of gypsum sand, its formation into dunes and their movement, as well as the stories of the larger geological events, can be learned at White Sands, the world's largest gypsum dune field.*"

Building from the WHSA Purpose and Significance statements, it is recommended that geologic and water resources be defined as "fundamental resources" at WHSA, warranting the highest level of preservation. The unique geologic features within the monument's boundaries are ultimately tied to both the historic and current geologic and hydrologic processes of the Tularosa Basin. It is the mission of the National Park Service at WHSA to preserve the world's largest gypsum dunefield and the resources of interest related to the enabling legislation and provide educational and recreational opportunities compatible with the protection of those resources for future generations.

The elements of a unique geologic history, an abundance of gypsum, an enclosed drainage system, a dry climate, and strong winds have combined to create this unique natural area. The outstanding geological and biological features, the superlative scenic values and recreational opportunities, and its location on a major highway (U.S. 70) make WHSA one of the most popular national park areas in the southwest United States.

Physical Resources Planning

This *Physical Resources Foundation Report* is designed to support development of the *Foundation Document* for WHSA and to be used as a reference for the *General Management Plan,* as needed. In accordance with the 2004 NPS Park Planning Program Standards, six discrete elements of planning are captured in six planning-related documents (Figure 1). This section outlines the individual elements of the NPS planning framework (National Park Service,

2004), including the *Foundation Document*, and better describes how this report fits into the framework.

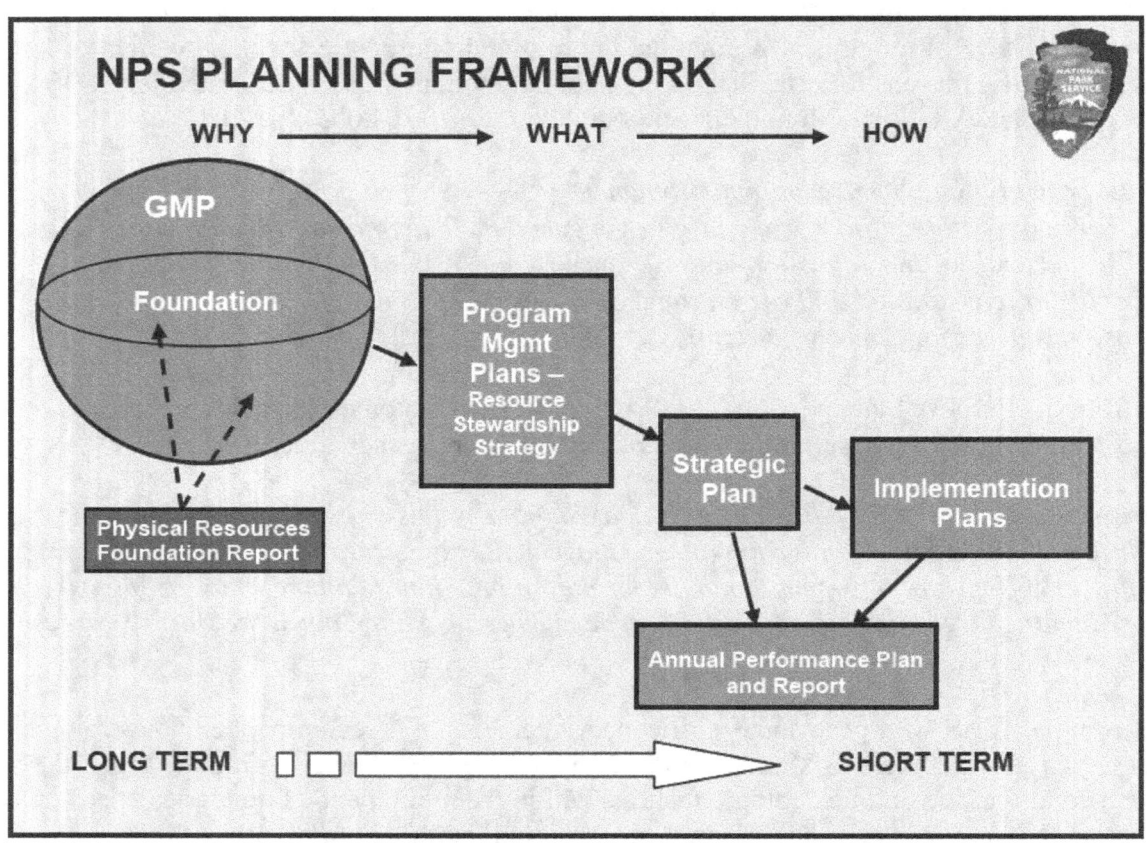

Figure 1. National Park Service Planning Framework.

The *Foundation for Planning and Management* document (Foundation Document) defines the legal and policy requirements that mandate the park's basic management responsibilities, and identifies and analyzes the resources and values that are fundamental to achieving the park's purpose or otherwise important to park planning and management.

The *General Management Plan* (GMP) uses information from the *Foundation Document* to define broad direction for resource preservation and visitor use in a park, and serves as the basic foundation for park decision-making, including long-term direction for desired conditions of park resources and visitor experiences.

The *Program Management Plan* tiers off the GMP, identifying and recommending the best strategies for achieving the desire resource conditions and visitor experiences presented in the GMP. Program planning serves as a bridge to translate the qualitative statements of desired conditions into measurable or objective indicators that can be monitored to assess the degree to which the desired conditions are being achieved. Based on the information obtained through the analysis, comprehensive strategies are developed to achieve the desired condition. The *Program Management Plan* for natural and cultural resources is the *Resource Stewardship Strategy*.

The *Strategic Plan* tiers off the *Program Management Plan* identifying the highest-priority strategies, including measurable goals that work toward maintaining and/or restoring the park's desired conditions over the next 3 to 5 years.

Implementation Plans tier off the *Strategic Plan* describing in detail (including methods, cost estimate, and schedules) the high-priority actions that will be taken over the next several years to help achieve the desired conditions for the park.

The *Annual Performance Plan and Report* measure the progress of projects from the *Implementation Plan* with objectives from the *Strategic Plan*.

This *Physical Resources Stewardship Report* is designed to address the geologic and water resource needs in WHSA's *Foundation Document* and will be helpful in preparing the monument's *General Management Plan*.

The primary objectives of this report are to:

1. Build upon the monument's purpose and significance statements and identify the *fundamental* physical resources critical to achieving WHSA's purpose and maintaining its significance.
2. Provide background information for WHSA's *fundamental* physical resources (current condition, related trends, and issues/threats).
3. Define the relevant laws and policies that support management decisions for the priority physical resources and identify stakeholder interest.

Location and Demography

The monument is located in south central New Mexico between the Sacramento and San Andres mountains in Otero and Don Ana counties. The monument is completely surrounded by the White Sands Missile Range and Holloman Air Force Base. The approximately 144,000-acre monument lies within the Tularosa Basin--an enclosed drainage system that contains numerous playa lakes and lies within the northern reaches of the Chihuahuan Desert (Figure 2). The lands within the monument are 100% fee title owned by the U.S. Government and managed by the National Park Service. The monument receives approximately 450,000 visitors each year (White Sands 2001-2005 Strategic Plan, 2000 [http://www.nps.gov/applications/parks/whsa/ppdocuments/Strategic Plan WHSA.htm]).

Alamogordo is the principal population center in the region; smaller communities include Tularosa and Carrizozo. In 2000, the regional population was reported at 60,357 and projected to reach 94,000 by 2040 (Livingston and Shomaker, 2002). The economy is centered on military bases in the area consisting of the White Sands Missile Range, Holloman Air Force Base, and part of Fort Bliss (Huff, 2004). A USGS topographic map and true color satellite image of the monument area are shown in Figure 3.

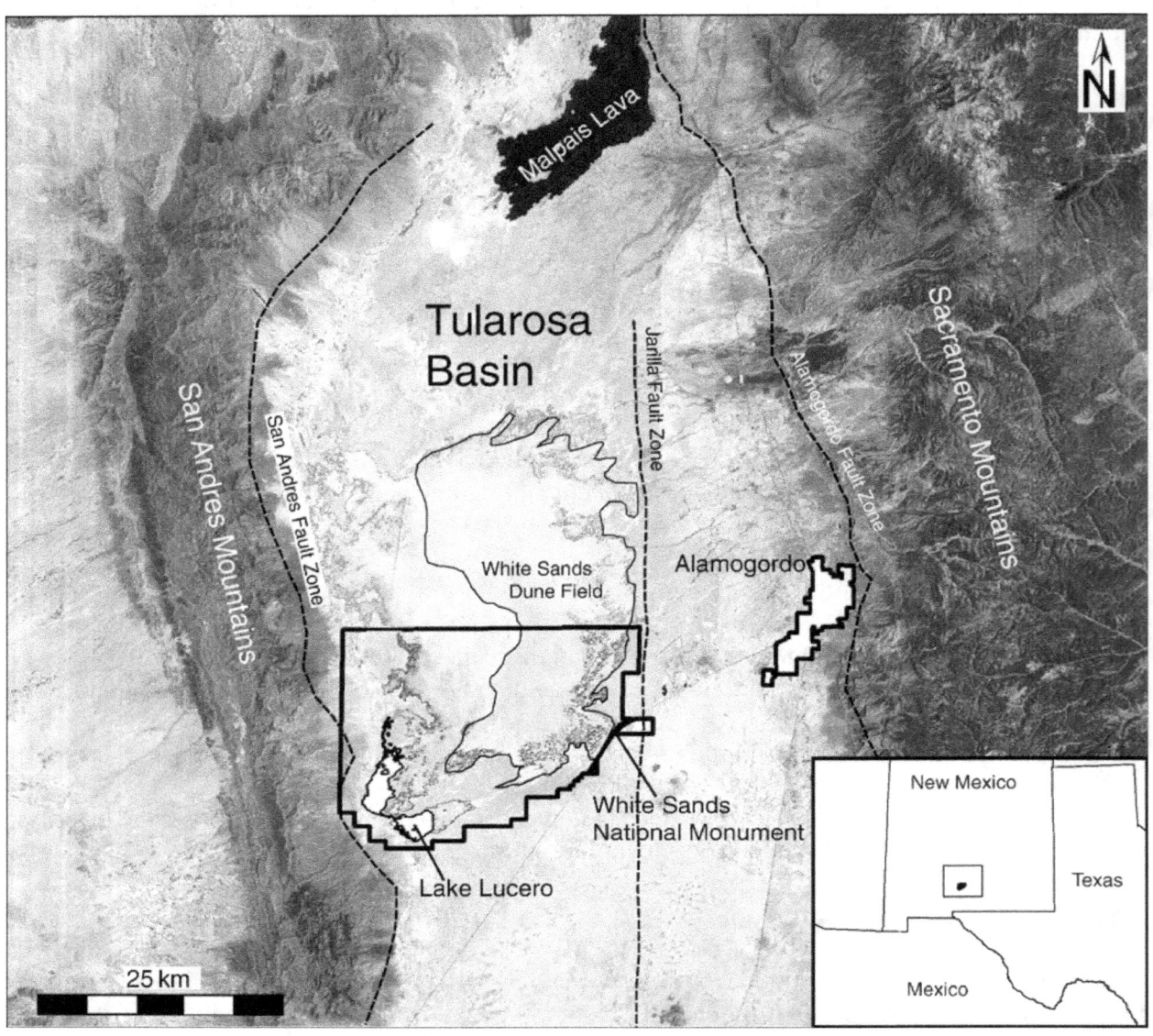

Figure 2. White Sand National Monument index map. The National Monument lies at the southern end of the Tularosa Basin within the Basin and Range physiographic province. The monument encompasses approximately 40% of the world's largest gypsum dunefield. Source: Kocurek et al. (2007).

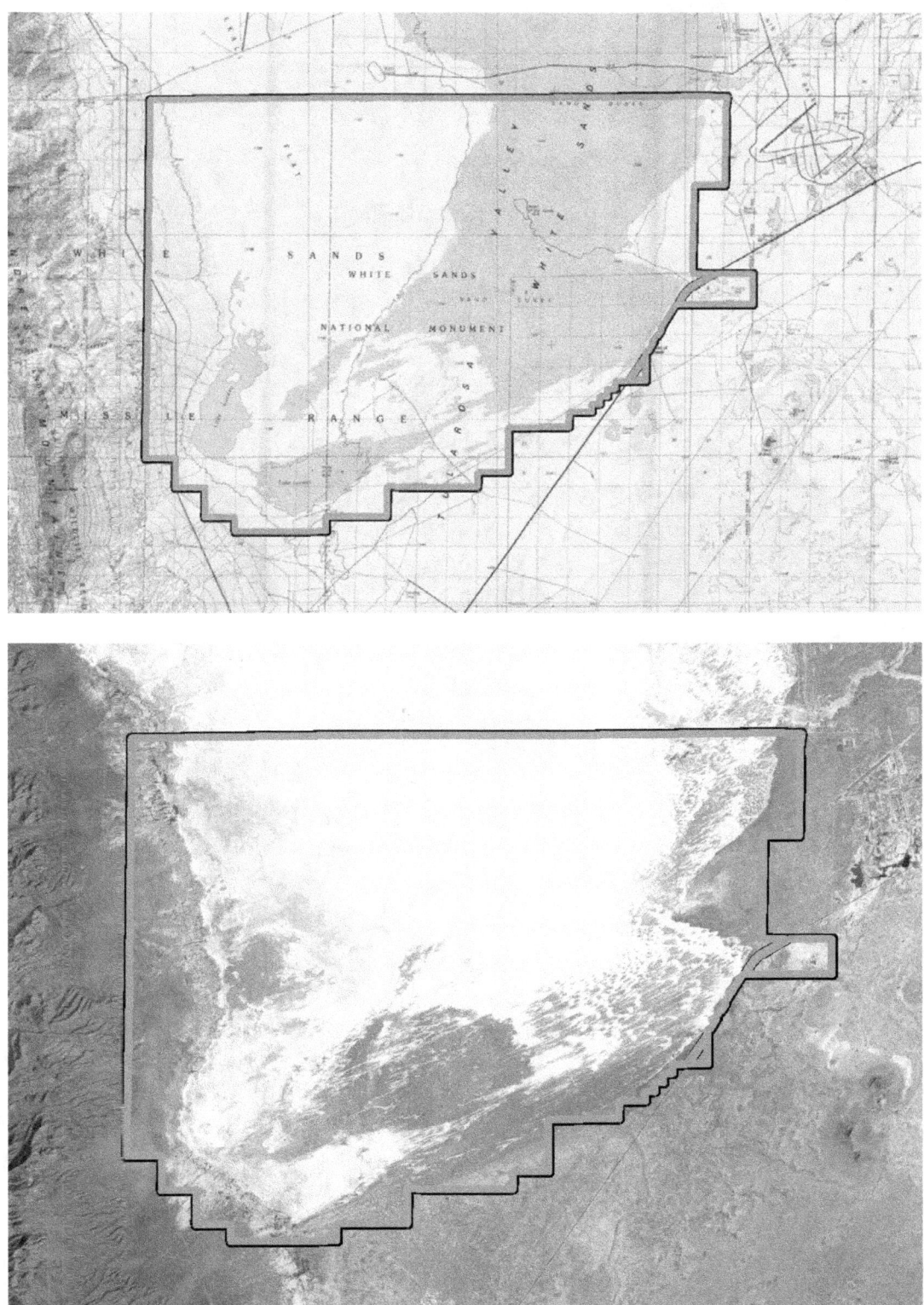

Figure 3. Topographic map (top) and true color satellite imagery (bottom) of White Sands National Monument. Source: ESRI online maps).

Description of Natural Resources

Climate

The high desert area of the monument is subject to harsh and sometimes rapidly changing climatic conditions. Summers are hot, averaging 96°F and 97°F in June and July, with air temperatures frequently exceeding 100°F. Winters are cool to cold with average minimums of 22°F and 23°F in December and January (from WHSA website: *http://www.nps.gov/whsa/climate-averages.htm*). White Sands is located approximately equidistant from two principal moisture sources, the Gulf of Mexico and the Sea of Cortez. The monument is influenced by tropical moisture from both sources during the summer monsoon season (Reid and Reiser, 2006). Little precipitation is associated with mid-latitude storm events; consequently it has only one rainy season -- the summer monsoon. Table 1 summarizes temperature and precipitation records for the monument. More detailed summaries of weather are available from the Chihuahuan Desert Inventory and Monitoring Network (Reid and Reiser, 2006; Davey et al., 2007).

Table 1. Temperature and precipitation data recorded at White Sands National Monument between 1/1/1939 to 12/31/1999 *(from Fryberger, 2001).*

	Jan	Feb	Mar	Apr	May	Jun	Jul	Aug	Sep	Oct	Nov	Dec	Annual
Average Max. Temperature (°F)	57	63	70.4	79.3	88	96.7	97	94.4	88.8	78.9	66.1	56.8	78
Average Min. Temperature (°F)	22.3	25.6	31.3	39.3	48.3	58.2	63.8	61.5	54	40.8	28	21.8	41.2
Average Total Precip. (inches)	0.53	0.34	0.3	0.28	0.38	0.72	1.43	1.71	1.32	0.87	0.42	0.68	8.97
Average Total Snow Fall (inches)	1	0.4	0.1	0	0	0	0	0	0	0	0.2	1.1	2.8
Average Snow Depth (inches)	0	0	0	0	0	0	0	0	0	0	0	0	0

Peak wind season occurs during the spring with southwest winds averaging about 23 miles per hour. During the winter, northerly and southerly winds are significant but not strong enough to permanently change the shapes of the dunes, which migrate consistently towards the northeast under the influence of the southwest winds. This wind regime appears to have been in place since the development of the dune field since there is no evidence of dune cross bedding for older wind regimes of a different average direction (Fryberger, 2001). Figure 4 includes rose diagrams depicting wind data collected at Holloman AFB.

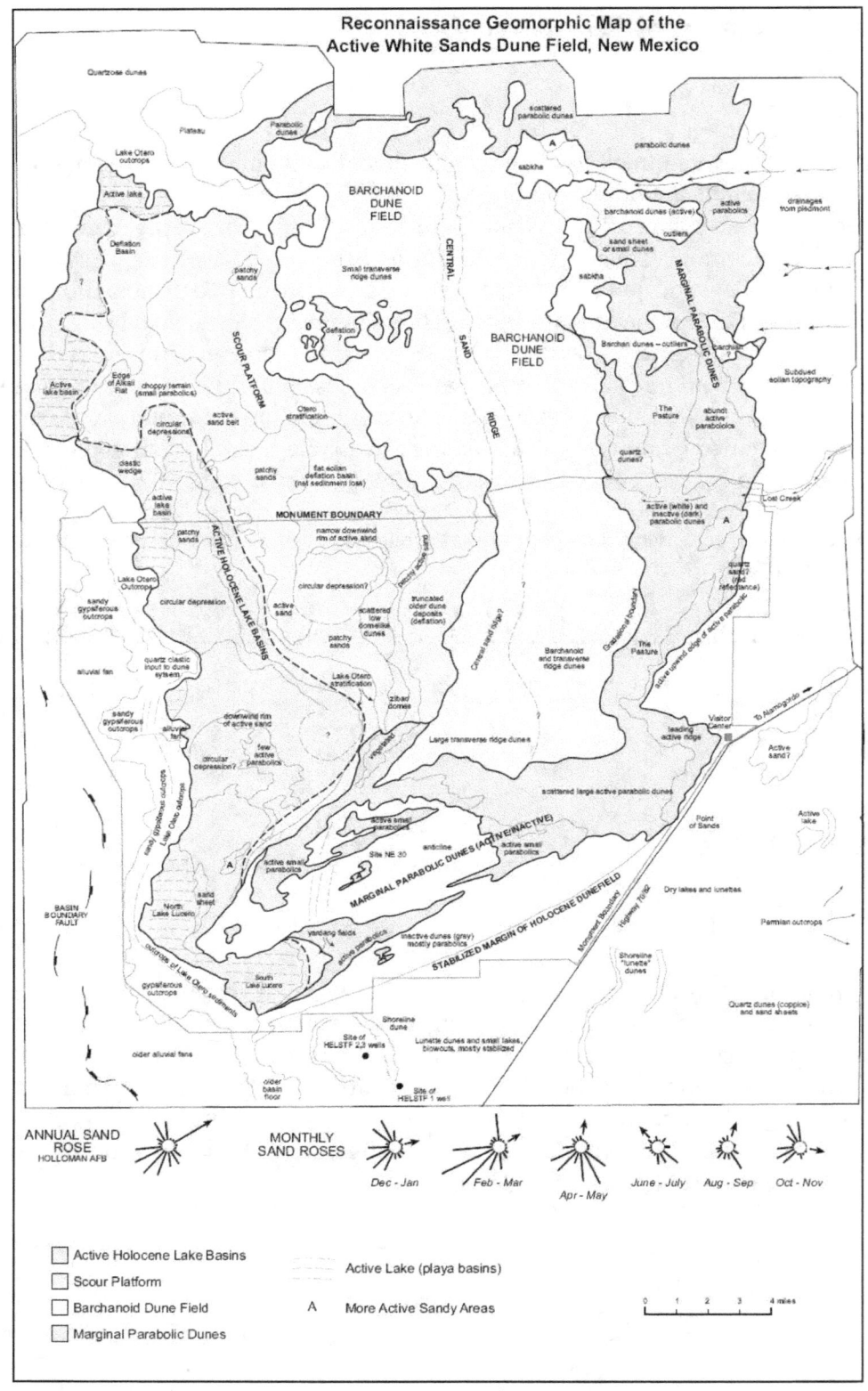

Figure 4. Dune type and major physiographic feature distribution associated with White Sands National Monument. From Shell U.K. Exploration and Production, Nov. 1999 (Fryberger, 2001 -- Monument boundary approximate).

Physiography

White Sands National Monument is situated in the Tularosa Basin of the Rio Grande Rift, and is flanked on the west by the San Andres Mountains and on the east by the Sacramento Mountains. The Tularosa Basin is a hydrologically closed basin. Run-off and surface water infiltrate basin sediments or collect in playa lakes. Like any bowl shaped structure, water collects in the center and eventually evaporates, leaving behind salt deposits. The monument is dominated by this process which created Lake Lucero and Alkali Flat. Winds, blowing preferentially from the south move the soft, gypsiferous sediments to form the monument's dune field. The 275-square-mile gypsum dune field extends northeastward from Lake Lucero and continues beyond the northern border of the monument.

Alkali Flat and Lake Lucero

Alkali Flat and Lake Lucero are remnants of the much larger glacial lake named Lake Otero that formed during the last ice age about 24,000 to 12,000 years ago. The Alkali Flat covers approximately 1,600 square miles. Lake Lucero, which occupies the topographically lowest area of the Tularosa Basin, is at the south end of a 30-mile string of playas (Allmendinger and Titus, 1973) and is the largest of the playas. The lake, or more appropriately playa, lies 3,890 feet above mean sea level and is approximately 60 feet below the dunes to the west. All the playas are sharply defined basins with abrupt and steep edges, nearly level floors and were formed by wind erosion. The presence of water varies depending on seasonal changes of inflow and evaporation. Because of the flat topography, a small water-level change has a large effect on the surface area of the ephemeral lake, which may cover about ten square miles.

Dune Field

The dune field is composed of primarily gypsum sands and covers 275 mi^2 with about 115 mi^2 located within White Sands National Monument. The dune field consists of a core of barchan dunes flanked to the north, east, and south by fields of parabolic dunes (Kocurek et al., 2007).

Geology

The Tularosa Basin is the northern portion of one of the largest basins in the Rio Grande Rift, the Tularosa-Hueco Basin (Chapin, 1971). At over 160 miles long and 30 miles wide, the basin covers approximately 6,000 mi^2. On the east, the Tularosa Basin is bounded by the Jicarilla, Sierra Blanca, and Sacramento mountains. The Otero Mesa bounds the basin's southern end. Chupadera Mesa and the Oscura, San Andres, Organ, and Franklin mountains form the west flanks of the basin (Meinzer and Hare, 1915).

Sediments in the basin were deposited in shallow inland seas that advanced and retreated across southern New Mexico throughout the Paleozoic Era. By the late Paleozoic, the sea levels were dropping and water circulation became restricted behind the reef deposits to the southeast (King and Harder, 1985). As the seas evaporated, large carbonate and evaporite deposits were left behind to form rock units such as the Permian-aged San Andres, Yeso and Abo formations. These formations are exposed as light-colored layers near the top of the San Andres Mountains and contain large amounts of gypsum which supplies the sands that form the dunes of White Sands.

With the onset of the Laramide Orogeny (mountain building episode) 70 million years ago, these units were uplifted into a broad dome. Beginning 10 million years ago, the center of this dome collapsed during formation of the Rio Grande Rift to create the Tularosa Basin. The sides of the original dome now form the San Andres and Sacramento mountain ranges that ring the basin (King and Harder, 1985).

More recently, extensive igneous activity such as the eruption of the Sierra Blanca volcano and the intrusives of the Jarilla, Cornudas, Sierra Blanca, Lone, and Tres Hermanos mountains have occurred (King and Harder, 1985) (Figure 5).

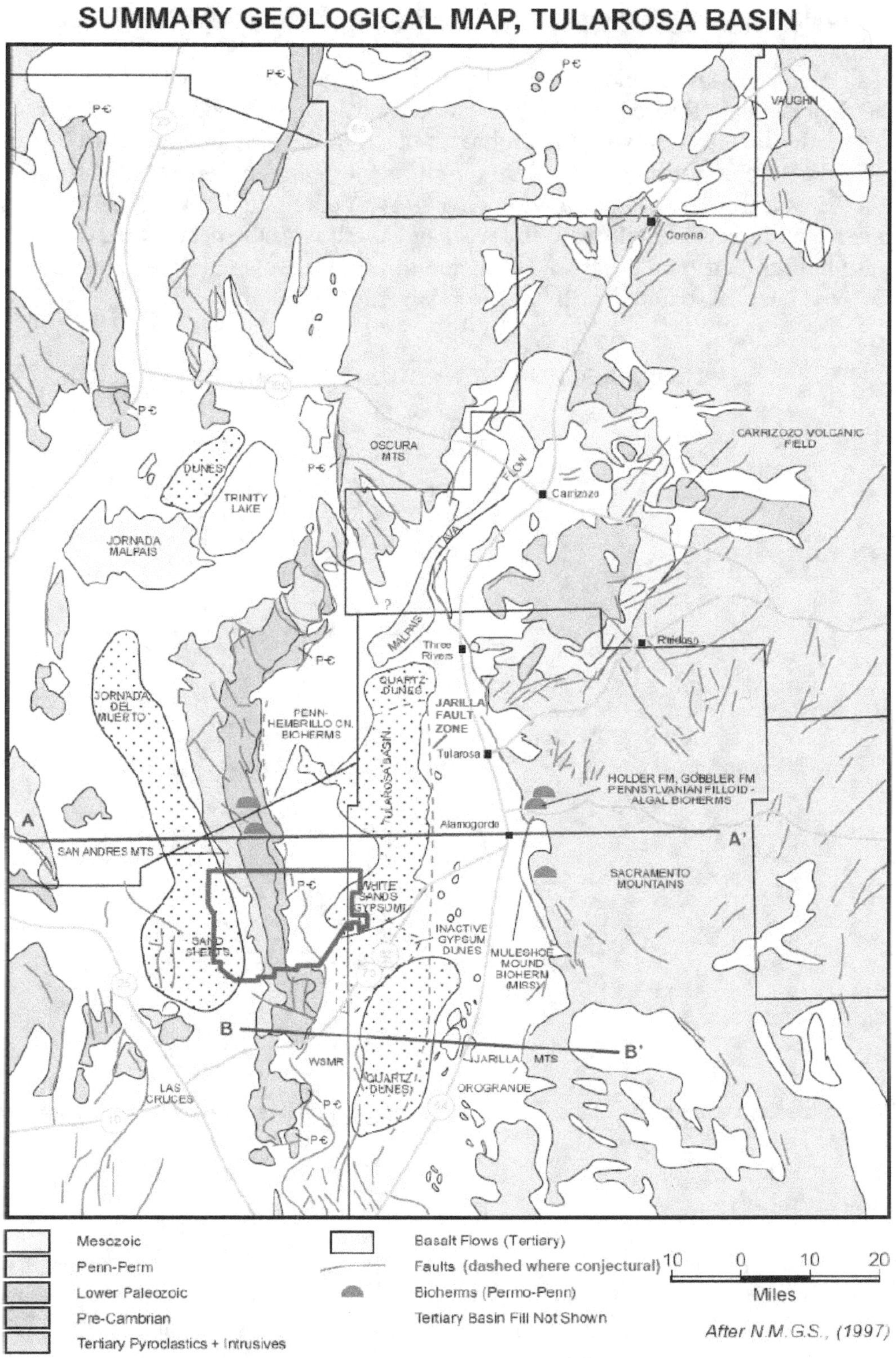

SUMMARY GEOLOGICAL MAP, TULAROSA BASIN

Figure 5. Geologic map of the Tularosa Basin and vicinity. Refer to Figure 7 for rock formation names *(from Fryberger, 2001).* Approximate location of Jarilla Fault Zone inferred from Figure 5 in *Finch, 2006.*

Structural Geology

The Tularosa Basin is a fault bounded internally drained depression in south-central New Mexico. The depression is formed by two half grabens or down dropped blocks. The two grabens are separated by the Jarilla Fault with the upthrown block to the east (Figure 6). In the area of the monument, the Jarilla Fault brings bedrock to the surface effectively separating basin fill sediments on the east from those on the west. Geophysical data (Healy et al., 1978) indicates basin asymmetry with the basin tilting to the west and south with the deepest portion of the basin on the western half graben. The Tularosa Basin and the Hueco Bolson to the south are two halves of a large tectonic basin associated with the Rio Grande Rift (Chapin, 1971).

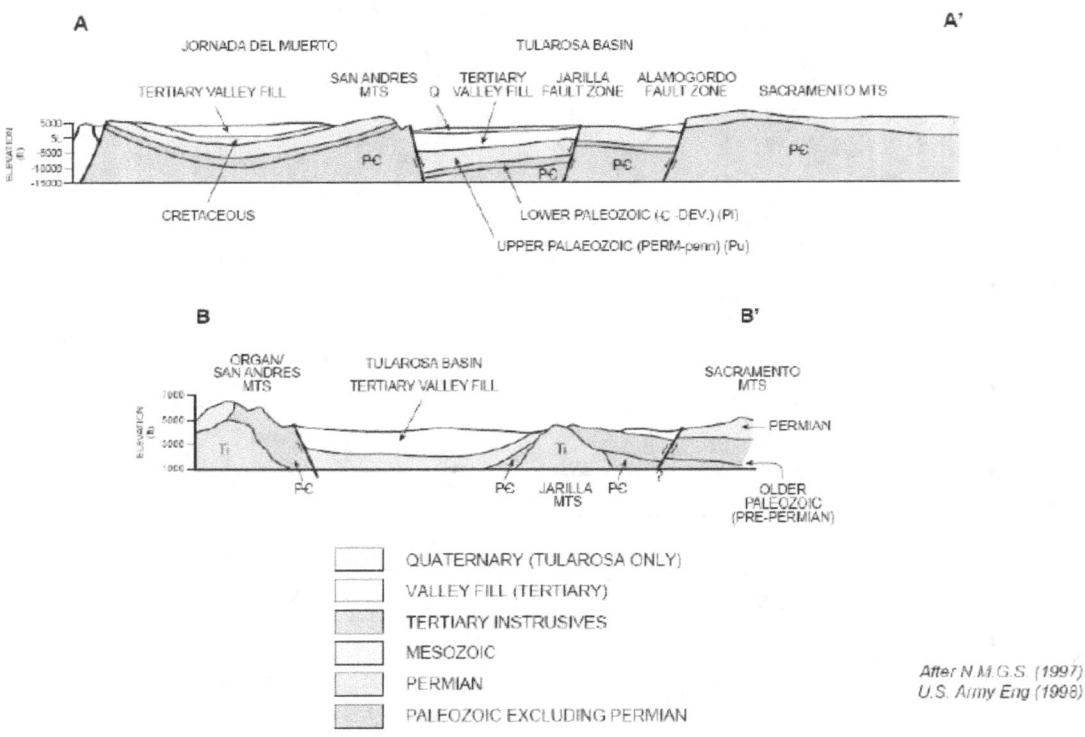

Figure 6. Generalized cross sections of the Tularosa Basin. Section lines are shown in Figure 5 *(from Fryberger, 2001).*

Stratigraphy/Lithology

Rocks in the Tularosa Basin were deposited during the Paleozoic through Cenozoic Eras. The uniqueness of White Sands as the largest gypsum dunefield in the world is directly related to the geologic history that preceded dune formation. The presence of shallow and sometimes restricted inland seas throughout most of the Paleozoic and Mesozoic Eras (Orr and Myers, 1986) was affected by both orogenic processes and rifting (Fryberger, 2001). Figure 7 summarizes the stratigraphy in context of the general tectonic history of the basin. The subsurface geology in the basin dates back to the Pre-Cambrian while surficial geology of the monument is dominated by Quaternary and Holocene sediments.

COLUMNAR SECTION
TULAROSA BASIN

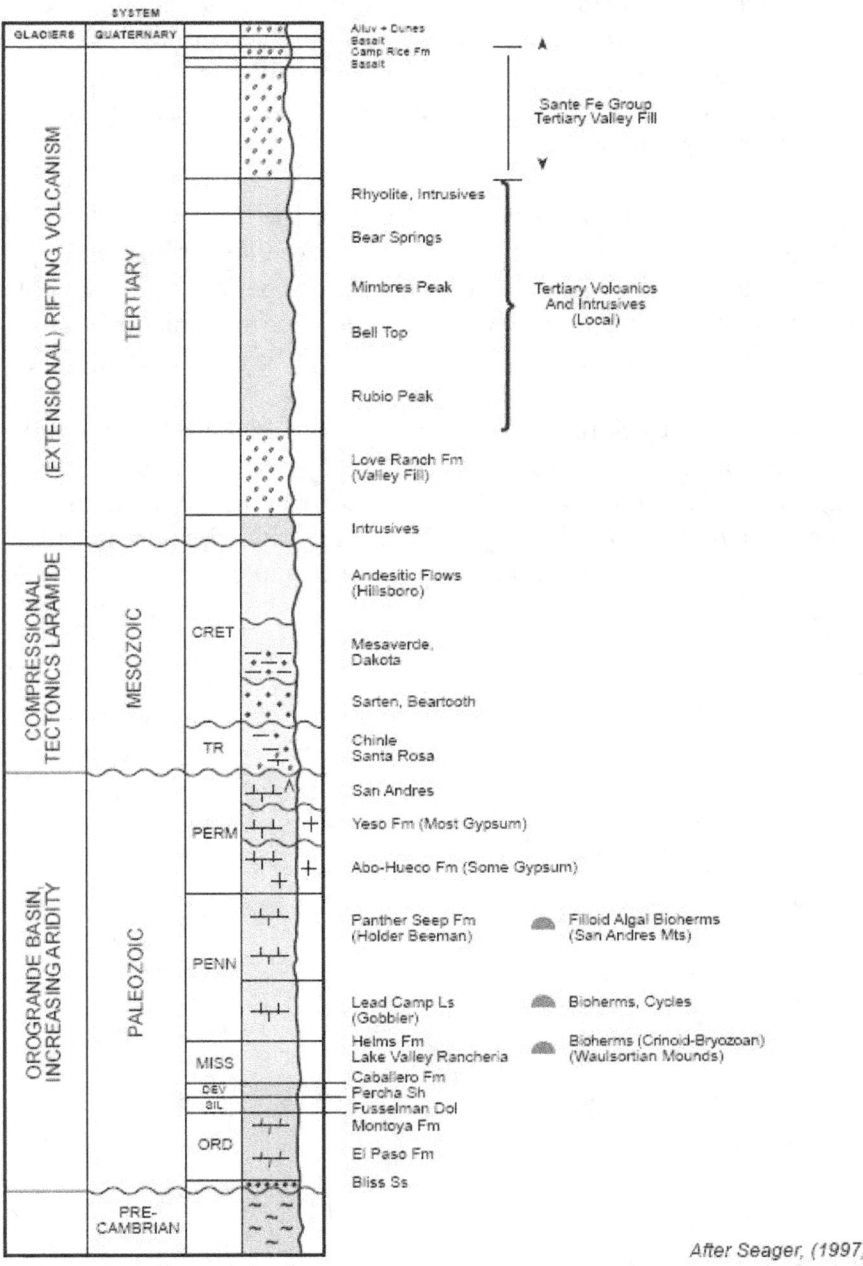

After Seager, (1997)

Figure 7. General stratigraphic column of the Tularosa Basin (*Seager et al., 1997 in Fryberger, 2001*).

Geologic Processes

Gypsum/Selenite Formation

The mineral gypsum, a hydrous form of calcium sulfate, is rarely found as sand because it is soluble in water. Gypsum--soft and lightly colored--frequently occurs interstratified with limestones and shales and will precipitate from saline solutions before halite (rock salt) (Hurlbut and Klein, 1977). Selenite is a form of gypsum (Figure 8) that yields large, occasionally colorless, transparent crystals (Hurlbut and Klein, 1977). The commonly observed amber coloring is due to organic acids within the crystals. Normally, dissolved gypsum would be transported by rivers to the sea. Since no river drains the Tularosa Basin, gypsum and other sediments remain trapped in the basin.

The gypsum that forms the white sands was eroded from the Permian rocks in the surrounding highlands and deposited at the bottom of Lake Otero. Lake Otero's size and hydrology was affected by the last glacial period. At the end of the glacial period, the lake contracted and evaporated. The exposed lake beds were eroded to produce fine white gypsum sand that through eolian processes later created the White Sand's dunefield (Szynkiewicz et al., 2008).

The gypsum sand is created by deflation of evaporite beds of Lake Otero and the younger playa lakes, primarily Lake Lucero—a remnant of Lake Otero (Kocurek et al., 2007). Gypsum dissolves in water into calcium ions and sulfate ions which recombine under evaporating conditions and precipitate out again into gypsum or anhydrite. Gypsum has many commercial uses; it is very common, and mined in sufficient quantities in other parts of the United States.

Figure 8. Amber selenite crystals at Lake Lucero (NPS Photo).

During wet periods, the evaporative process along the shore of Lake Lucero and the Alkali Flat results in the formation of beds of selenite crystals, some up to three feet long although monument staff have reported only smaller crystals after recent wet periods. When the dominant wind from the southwest blows across the dried up playa of Lake Lucero and the Alkali Flat, finer silts and clays are blown away, a process called deflation, leaving the crystals exposed. Weathering breaks them up by:

1. Large temperature differences between day and night stressing the mineral
2. Freezing and thawing of water which seeps along the cleavage planes
3. Dissolution by water working preferentially along the cleavage planes

Transport or movement of grains begins with wind speeds between 10 and 20 mph, depending on grain size. There are two principle manners in which sand grains are moved by the wind:

1. Suspension — particles are kept aloft by eddies and updrafts.
2. Saltation — particles hop and bounce over the ground.

As sand grains are moved by the wind, they are reduced in size by frequent collisions with other grains and the land surface. The softness and perfect cleavage of gypsum aids this process. Sand refers to size, not composition. Sand is defined as any particle between 0.06251 and 2.0 mm in diameter. Particles less than 0.06251 mm are called silt and clay and those over 2.0 mm are called granules and pebbles. In qualitative terms, sand is defined as any particle light enough to be moved by wind, but too heavy to be held in suspension in the air.

The Geoindicators Scoping Report notes that although very little new gypsum is forming today, wind erosion of the gypsum-bearing sediments of ancient Lake Otero continues, along with the breakdown of the small gypsum crystals to produce sand (KellerLynn, 2003). This process, rather than contribution from Lake Lucero sediments, is the main process feeding the most active portions of the dune field. The contribution of gypsum from Lake Lucero is limited by dampness, mud, and evaporite cementation within the lake bed. Areas immediately downwind of the lake exhibit signs of scour as partly lithified gypsum dunes are eroded. Whether or not the dune field is growing or shrinking remains to be seen, however it is known that the leading edge of the dune field is advancing to the northeast (Fryberger, 2001).

Dune Formation

Deposition of sand occurs whenever the wind slackens such as in the lee of plants or other obstacles. Moving particles that encounter a softer surface (such as loose sand) during saltation (bouncing along) will also slow down and accumulate.

As the sand grains accumulate in to dunes, they bounce up the gentle windward side of the dune, creating ripples on the surface. At the steep leading edge of the dune, sand builds up until gravity pulls the sand down the slip face, moving the dune forward. As sand accumulates, the dune becomes an obstruction to wind movement that further contributes to dune formation. Dune types and general characteristics are discussed on the following page.

Continued dune formation and migration is primarily dependent upon gypsum supply and wind. Where dunes form is dependent upon the factors listed above. Dunes would not form without an internally drained Tularosa Basin that allows for the evaporative processes that produces selenite, weathering processes that break down selenite crystals, and a wind regime that subsequently transports gypsum sand. Surface water and groundwater that support vegetation are important controls on where dunes occur and the rate and frequency of movement if the dunes.

Erosion

Weathering due to wind and water is the principle driver of landform formation within the monument. In general, winds out of the west and southwest transport newly formed sediments (broken down selenite crystals) from playas and deposit them as dunes. Subsequent dune movements is also driven primarily by wind.

Along the western edge of the monument, water is responsible for the formation of Bajadas-- piedmont landforms consisting of coalescing alluvial fans. Bajadas have braided streams and distinct plant and animal communities (KellerLynn, 2003).

Distinctive erosional hills called yardangs and plant and crystal pedestals that occur in the monument also result primarily from erosion and deposition due to prevailing winds.

Dune Types and Sizes

Four types of dunes are known to occur in the monument:

1. **Dome.** The first dunes to form downwind of Lake Lucero are low mounds of sand.
2. **Transverse.** In areas with ample sand, barchan dunes join together into long ridges of sand.
3. **Barchan.** Crescent-shaped dunes form in areas with strong winds and a limited supply of sand.
4. **Parabolic.** On the dune field edges, plants anchor the arms of barchans and invert their shape.

Figure 4 shows the distribution of major dune types in and around the monument. Figure 9 depicts the four major dune types that occur in the monument.

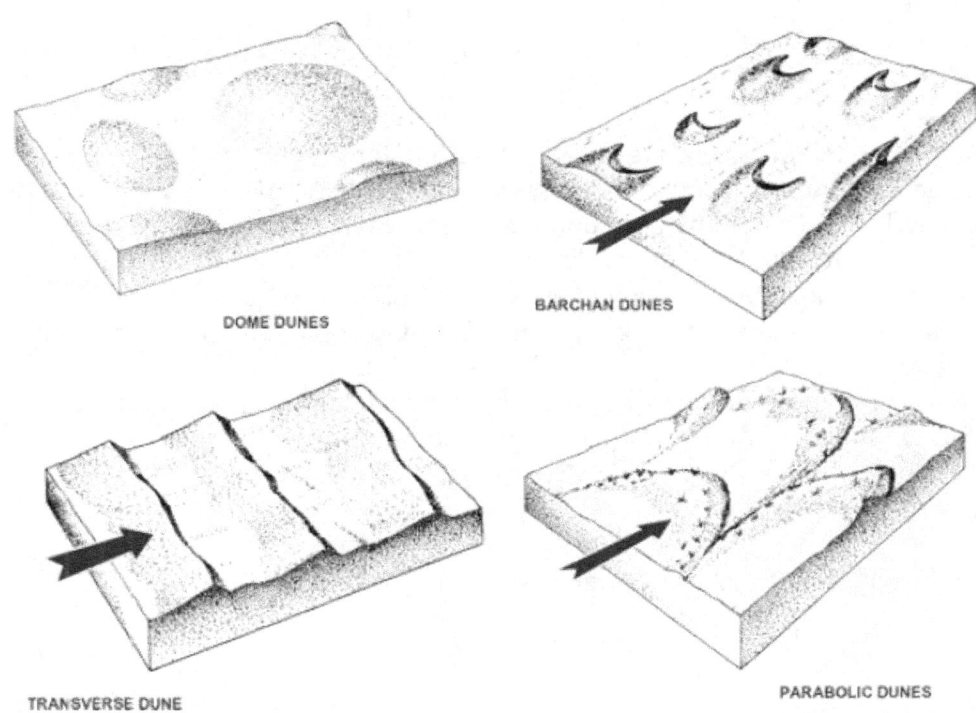

DOME DUNES

BARCHAN DUNES

TRANSVERSE DUNE

PARABOLIC DUNES

Figure 9. Dune types of White Sands National Monument. Arrows show prevailing wind direction (McKee, 1979).

There is a noticeable lack of dome dunes in the monument (KellerLynn, 2008). However, the monument brochure includes an illustration of dome dunes and discusses them as part of the landscape. Also, McKee and Douglass, 1971, note the occurrence of dome dunes and report rates of movement of these and other dune types (Table 2).

Table 2. Dune movement rates by dune type. Average rates derived from McKee and Douglass, 1971.

Dune Type (in order of formation from upwind to downwind)	Average rate of movement (ft/year)
Dome	32.75
Transverse/ Barchanoid ridge	7.5
Barchan	8.25
Parabolic	3.5
Eastern margin Parabolics	2.5

Interdunes

The interdune areas at White Sands, like the dunes, exist in several varieties. Groundwater is often within a few feet of the surface and has widely varying salinities depending on location and season. This aspect, along with sub-environments created by the forms of the dunes result in a wide variety of interdune types. Much of the flora and fauna depend on the interdune areas where moisture and nutrient levels and protection from wind provide a favorable microclimate (Fryberger, 2001).

Wind and sand flow conditions in the interdune areas differ from in the dunes due to their location. Wind speed and direction are commonly more variable in interdunes than on dunes due to turbulence and wind deflection caused by surrounding dunes. The winds are commonly weaker in interdunes although it is not uncommon for interdunes to experience strong winds if the wind is funneled through a gap between two dunes. This is a common condition within barchan dunes. It is common for rates of sand deposition to be quite slow or for scour to occur in interdune areas immediately downwind of slip faces. This is due to trapping of sand by the dune slip faces. This can cause scour to occur where the wind flow, which has had much of its sand removed by the slip face, reattaches on the downwind, interdune surface.

Types of Interdunes

Fryberger (2001) classifies interdunes in four categories:

1. Erosional
2. Dry
3. Damp-wet (freshwater)
4. Evaporitic

Interdune classifications based on water are dynamic. A given interdune may change in area due to rainfall events or movement of surface or groundwater affecting the area. The current conditions on the surface represent a snapshot in the history of the interdune.

Lake (Playa) Lucero – Surface Sediments

The surface of Lake Lucero contains white powdery minerals that form as surface water evaporates. The primary component is calcium sulfate, or gypsum, and there are lesser amounts of sodium chloride (common table salt) and magnesium sulfate (Epsom salt). Also present are larger crystalline forms of these minerals. Calcium sulfate may be found as selenite and sodium chloride may be found as halite. These larger crystals form when groundwater, heavily laden with dissolved gypsum, moves upward to the surface of Lake Lucero through capillary action. As the water approaches the playa surface, it evaporates and selenite and halite crystals form in the mud just beneath the surface.

The surface crust, along with non-gypsiferous clay and silt washed into Lake Lucero during rainstorms eventually breaks down into fine particles and is moved by the wind. Allmendinger and Titus (1973) reports that material from this crust is so fine that winds often carry the sediments thousands of feet above ground level before depositing them beyond the White Sands dune field. This suggests that some of the sediments from Lake Lucero do not contribute to dune replenishment.

Lake Otero

Lake Otero formed during the last Ice Age (about 24,000 to 12,000 years ago) under much cooler and wetter climatic conditions than today. Higher precipitation rates led to the formation of the 1,600-square-mile Lake Otero. The precipitation also led to the dissolution of gypsum (calcium sulfate), salt (sodium chloride), and other soluble minerals from the Yeso and Abo-Hueco formations (Figure 7) in the surrounding mountains. These sediments were subsequently transported via run-off and deposited in Lake Otero.

For perhaps 20,000 years, Lake Otero occupied the Tularosa Basin. Silt, clay, and millions of tons of dissolved gypsum were washed from the mountains into the lake. About 12,000 years ago the climate changed again. With the end of the Ice Age, less rain fell on the mountains and warming temperatures began to dry up Lake Otero.

Figure 10 shows the distribution of younger geologic units in the vicinity of White Sands. The distribution of younger sand deposits indicate that the prevailing wind blew out of the southwest.

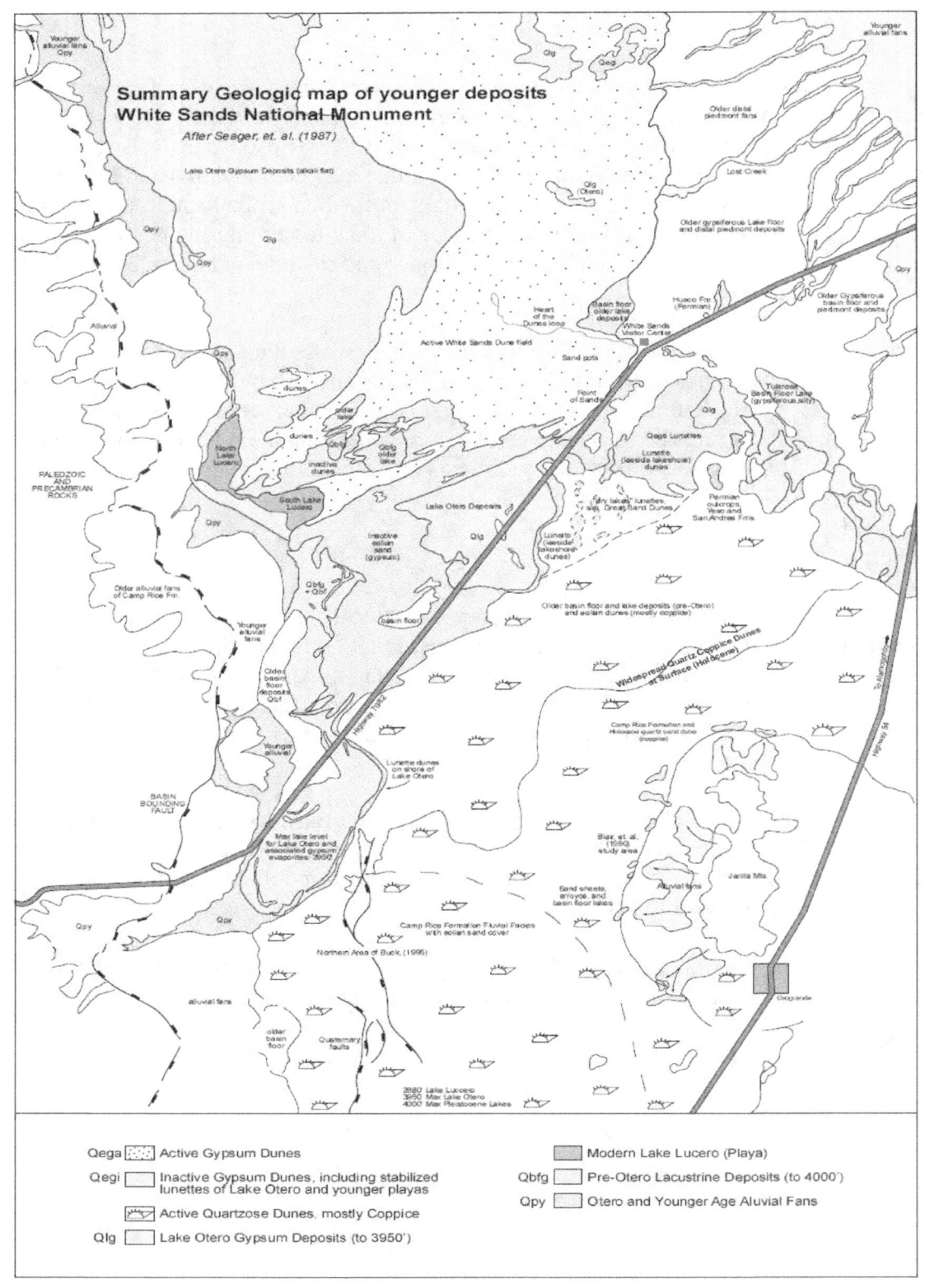

Figure 10. Geologic Map of the younger deposits near White Sands National Monument (after Seager et al., 1987 – Monument boundary approximate). Colored portions of the map emphasize the younger deposits mapped by Seager, et al. as contemporaneous with Lake Otero and later deposition.

20

Soils

The soil regime of White Sands National Monument is dominated by mineral soils associated with arid conditions. The soils in the monument are gypsum rich and host sparse yet highly diverse vegetation (KellerLynn, 2003). Figure 11 shows the distribution of general soil types within the monument.

Soil Crusts

Soil crusts occupy an intermediate ecological position between active dunes and heavily vegetated surfaces. Biological soil crusts consist of hydrophobic filaments of cyanobacteria and microfungi that wind through the upper two or three millimeters of soil binding soil particles together into aggregates. Filaments of cyanobacteria are hydrophobic, so crusts made of cyanobacteria promote lateral redistribution of water. That is, the horizontal-laying crusts impede the infiltration of water. These aggregates create surfaces for nutrient transformations. Physical crusts are inorganic and caused by features such as platy soil surface particles, an accumulation of salt, or a rainfall induced decrease in pore space (Rosentreter et al., 2007). Soil crusts play a critical role in dune stability (Guo et al., 2008).

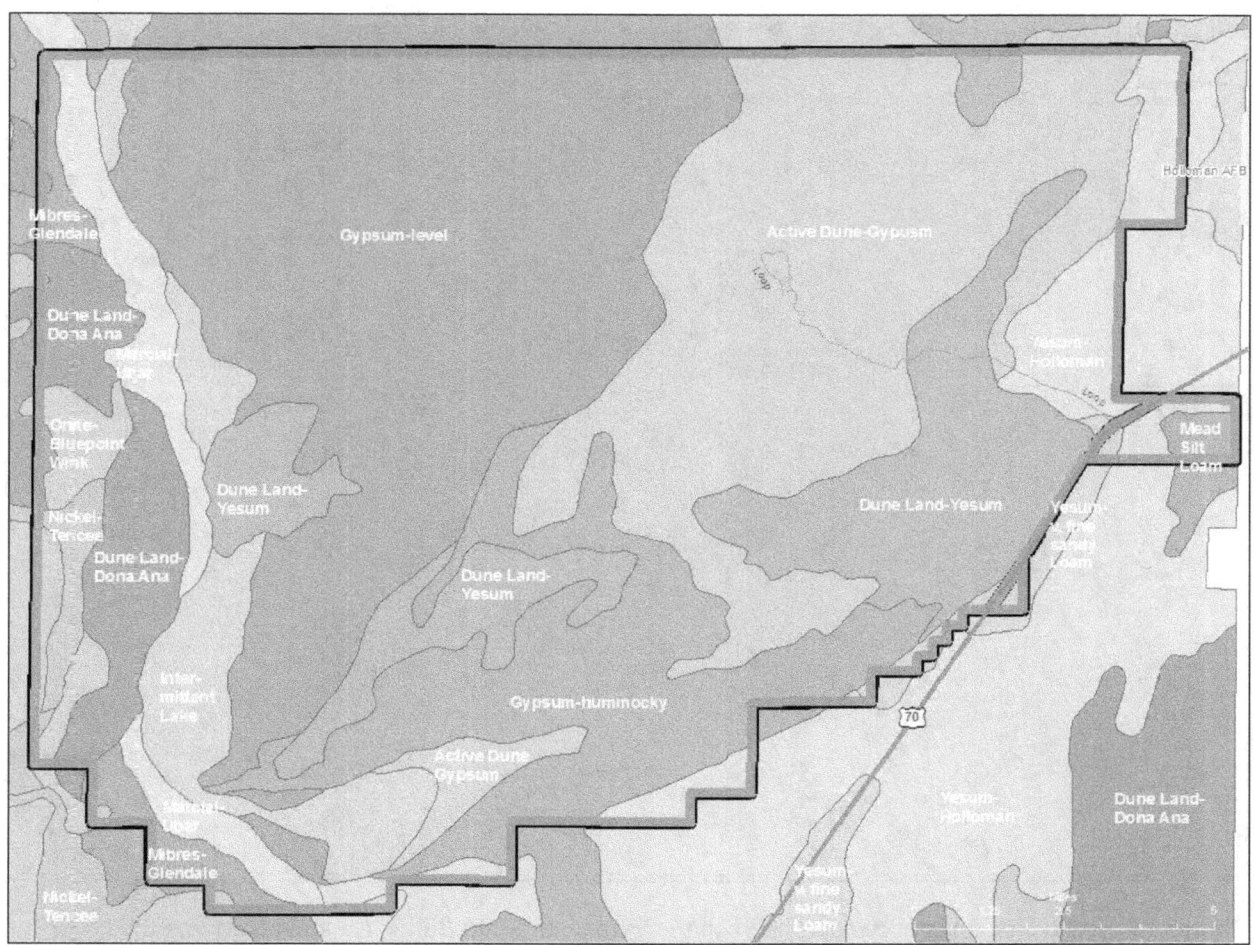

Figure 11. Soil types of White Sands National Monument (NPS GIS data supplied by Whites Sands National Monument).

21

Hydrogeology

Watersheds

According to the NPS Management Policies, the NPS will manage watersheds as complete hydrologic systems, and will minimize human disturbance to the natural upland processes that deliver water, sediment, and woody debris to streams (National Park Service, 2006).

Watersheds are delineated by the U.S. Geological Survey using a nation-wide system based on surface hydrologic features. This system divides the country into 21 regions, 222 sub regions, 352 accounting units, and 2,262 cataloguing units. A hierarchical hydrologic unit code (HUC) consisting of 2 digits for each level in the hydrologic unit system is used to identify any hydrologic area. The 6-digit accounting units and the 8-digit cataloguing units are generally referred to as basin and sub-basin, respectively. HUC's serve as the backbone for the country's hydrologic delineation. Within the HUC classification system, WHSA is located in the Rio Grande – Tularosa Valley sub-basin (13050003) of Region 13 (Figure 12).

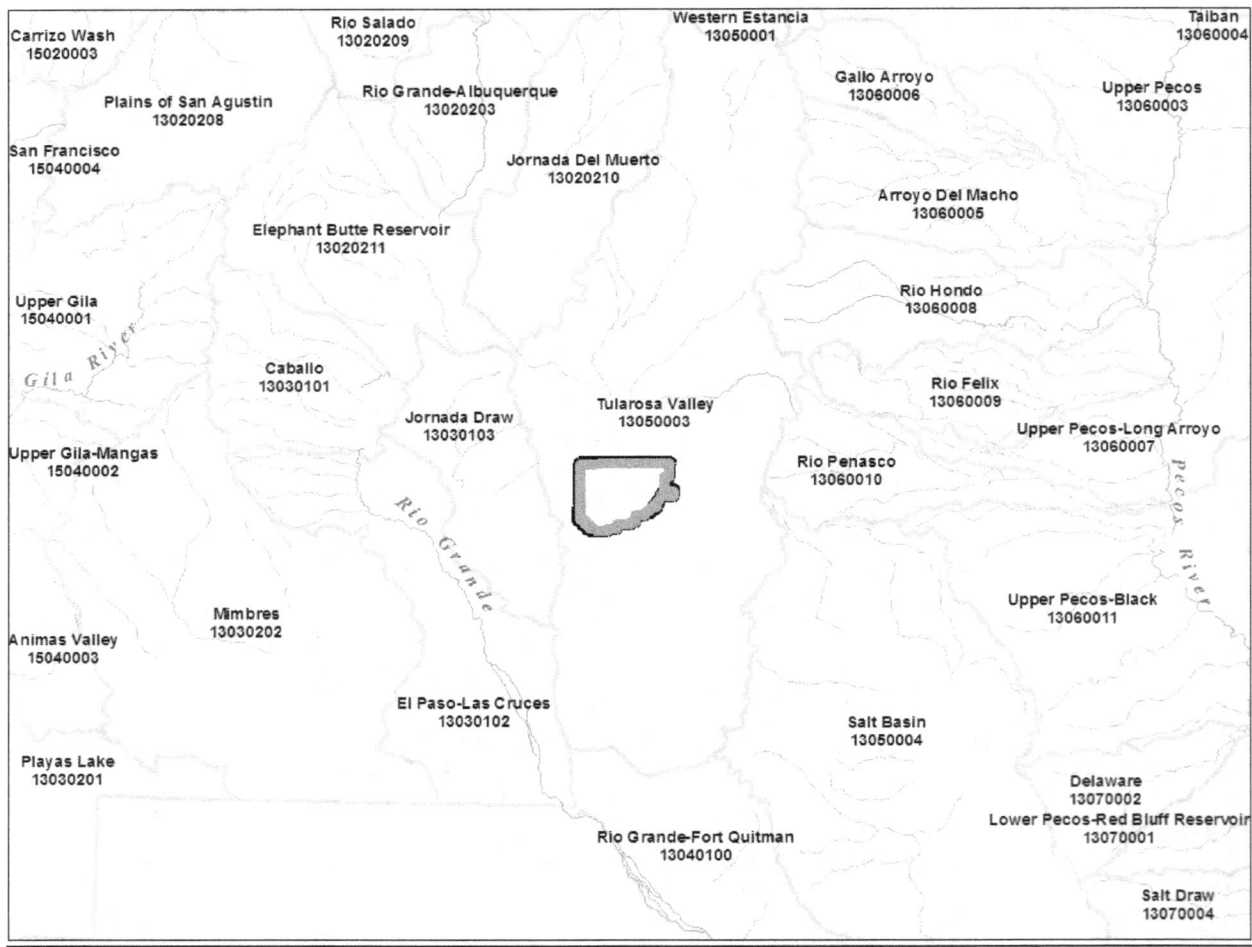

Figure 12. Hydrologic units and major rivers in the vicinity of White Sands National Monument (U.S. Geological Survey, 2009).

For the purpose of calculating the storm water runoff contribution to groundwater recharge, the U.S. Geologic Survey has identified 46 subbasins or watersheds that drain the highlands surrounding the Tularosa Basin, 20 of which are listed as "near White Sands" (Waltemeyer, 2001). Changing land use in any of these subbasins, but especially the nearest subbasins, could impact surface runoff or groundwater recharge. Storm-water runoff, altered by road construction or other activities, may pose a threat to monument resources. Threat assessments require basic watershed information. Pertinent data for the 20 nearest subbasins are listed in Table 3.

Table 3. Basic watershed information to assess potential threats posed by runoff and erosion. Major watersheds in the western Tularosa Basin that contribute surface runoff to WHSA, summary of watershed data and estimated yield, from Waltemeyer (2001).

Stream Name	Drainage Area (mi²)	Mean Annual Precipitation (in/yr)	Mean Elevation (ft-msl)	USGS Estimated Mean Annual Streamflow (acre-ft/yr)
Oak Canyon	8.94	14.85	5,717	203
Soledad Canyon	15.6	15.88	6,335	485
Sotol Creek	13.1	14.32	5,646	319
Unnamed arroyo	12.2	11.91	4,898	217
Bear Canyon	15.4	11.8	5,741	290
Little San Nicolas Canyon	7.35	12.0	6,155	109
Ash Canyon	7.60	13.81	6,352	145
San Andres	8.9	15.63	5,845	217
Mayberry Canyon	11.5	15.49	5,695	304
Deadman Canyon	16.1	14.33	5,576	427
Lost Man Canyon	10.2	12.88	5,954	188
Hembrillo Canyon	17.2	12.00	5,669	348
Grandview Canyon	2.82	12.00	5,928	29
Sulfur Canyon	30.3	12.04	5,770	746
Ash Canyon	4.2	12.08	6,352	51
Workman Canyon	5.99	12.66	6,141	94
Cottonwood Canyon	45.3	13.73	5,791	1,600
Rhoades Canyon	39.7	14.57	6,185	1,477
Good Fortune Canyon	24.0	15.34	6,228	811
Thurgood Canyon	37.2	13.8	5,589	1,231

Surface Water

Precipitation and the resulting runoff in the vicinity of White Sands generally follow surface and subsurface drainage systems to numerous playa lakes including Lake Lucero. The Sacramento Mountains receive twice as much precipitation as the San Andres Mountains because the Sacramento Mountains are higher in elevation. Snowmelt in the Sacramento Mountains sustains perennial streams at the mountain fronts. Precipitation in the San Andres Mountains occurs mainly as rainfall and arroyos draining the mountains flow only during storm events. The arroyos have been impacted by road construction and development. Culverts and other flow diversions concentrate flow and threaten archeological resources (KellerLynn, 2003).

Major streams in the vicinity of the monument include Salt Creek, Tularosa Creek, Malpais Creek, Barrel Spring, Brazel Lake and Lost River, of which the Lost River is the only stream that occasionally flows onto monument property. Located in the northeast portion of the monument, this stream originates outside the monument on DOD property, is perennial in the DOD reach and hosts a native pupfish. This stream, like other streams and wetlands located on the Jarilla fault, is sustained by groundwater. In addition, this stream, as well as all surface water in the basin, is heavily impacted by evaporation. The reach on NPS property is ephemeral and surface water that flows into the monument is blocked by dunes on the northeastern boundary (Barud-Zubillaga, 2000).

The dominant surface water feature at WHSA is Lake Lucero, a hypersaline, ephemeral playa occupying the lowest topographical point in the basin. During occasional rainy seasons the lake forms, but disappears during dry seasons. Barud-Zubillaga (2000) describes it as a groundwater discharge area, noting that the water table is near the elevation of the lake bed. Evaporation is a large part of the hydrologic balance of the groundwater system. Surface water and groundwater in the basin flow toward the playa.

Groundwater

Zones of Precipitation Runoff, and Percolation

For discussions of recharge and groundwater contribution to the basin fill aquifer, the topography of the Tularosa Basin can be divided into several hydrologic zones, as follows: (1) The mountain uplands, with heavy precipitation, heavy flood discharge, and a small perennial stream flow; (2) the upper portion or apex of the alluvial fans with low precipitation similar to the basin center, little runoff, and heavy percolation; (3) an area of dense clay soil with little precipitation, considerable runoff, small capillary adsorption and little percolation; (4) the interior gypsiferous plain which has minimum precipitation, little runoff, great capacity for capillary adsorption and considerable percolation through sinkholes; (5) the alkali flats with minimum precipitation, no run-off, little adsorption or percolation, and maximum evaporation (Meinzer and Hare, 1915).

Recharge of the groundwater in the basin is primarily by infiltration from runoff through the upper porous zone of the coalesced alluvial fans (bajadas) and debris slopes, the sink holes of the interior gypsiferous plain, and through the gypsum and quartz sands.

Regional Aquifers

The basin-fill aquifer of the Tularosa Basin, like many basins in the western U.S., is characterized by low recharge rates and long residence time. Sediments and dissolved minerals from the surrounding highlands have filled the basin since the onset of the Rio Grande Rift (Chapin, 1971). Coarse sediments shed from the surrounding highlands interfinger with the fine-grained fluvial and lake deposits of the basin center. Groundwater enters the basin through alluvial fans at the mountain flanks. Recent chemical and microbial evidence suggest that a deep geothermal source contributes to the aquifer (Schulze-Makuch, 2002). Some groundwater leaves the basin to the south, flowing into the Hueco Bolson, an important water supply for the city of El Paso (EL Paso Water Utilities, 2004). Most of the sediments in the bolson are saturated with saline water (Orr and Myers, 1986). Freshwater supplies are primarily found at the basin edges and more saline waters toward the center.

A major controlling structural feature of the basin fill aquifer is the Jarilla Fault. This north-south trending fault effectively divides the aquifer in two. Groundwater from the eastern subbasin flows westward over the bedrock high associated with the Jarilla Fault. Groundwater flow models, used for regional planning, assume that most of this water evaporates and contributes very little to the western subbasin (Finch, personal communication, 2009). However, the proximity of the fault to several perennial water sources (Brazel Lake, Barrel Springs and the Lost River) suggest that groundwater from the eastern subbasin is important in maintaining these features.

Local Aquifer

Groundwater that supports the hydrologic function of the playa and dune system is supplied by a regional groundwater gradient that transmits water from the surrounding mountains to the playas at the basin center. The process is complicated by the presence of the north-south trending Jarilla Fault located along the eastern boundary of WHSA. The eastern side of the fault has moved upward relative to the western block and has brought bedrock to or very near the surface, effectively separating the two sides of the basin fill aquifer. From where the fault intersects the surface the geologic formations dip to the east. Groundwater moving from the Sacramento Mountains westward into the basin is brought to the surface by these rising beds where it discharges as springs and wetlands primarily on Department of Defense property to the east of WHSA. Climate forces place heavy evaporation pressure on these resources. Some current groundwater flow models assume all this water evaporates and therefore presumes these resources would not contribute to water resources in the western basin. However, groundwater from the eastern side of the basin may not all evaporate and may contribute to recharge of groundwater resources in the western side. Groundwater from the eastern sub-basin may play a role in maintaining groundwater levels in the western sub-basin.

Groundwater elevations measured in the observation wells in the monument indicate that the water table is higher than might be expected based upon regional groundwater gradients. The observation wells are completed in a clay layer rich in organic material that underlies the dune field (Barud-Zubillaga, 2000). There has been speculation that this indicates a "perched" water table; however there are no data to suggest that sediments directly below the clay layer are not saturated. Nonetheless, the high water levels present an interesting puzzle and perhaps point to a disconnection between the regional aquifer and the local aquifer (Huff, 2005).

Regional Flow

Streamflow in the Tularosa Basin infiltrates through streambeds into the basin fill aquifer at or near the mountain fronts. Streamflow is a substantial part of the recharge for the aquifer. Streamflow differs substantially between the streams draining the Sacramento Mountains and the San Andres Mountains (Waltemeyer, 2001). Estimates of streamflow and potential recharge by the U.S. Geological Survey put the contribution from the Sacramento Mountains at 47,800 acre-feet and from the San Andres Mountains at 21,000 acre-feet. Recharge from streamflow from the eastern highlands is more than twice the streamflow from the western highlands.

The higher precipitation in the Sacramento Mountains causes greater recharge and debris fan construction on the west side of these mountains than on the eastern side. This combined with basin tilting create regional groundwater flow from northeast to the southwest (Huff, 2005).

Lensing

Basin sediments consist of interfingering coarse sediments shed from surrounding uplands and fine-grained stream and lake sediments. The coarse layers have greater porosity and allow groundwater to move relatively faster while the finer deposits retard the rate of groundwater movement. The faster movement of groundwater means less contact with soluble minerals, less dissolved solids, and better water quality. In some areas, these coarse beds extend far into the basin providing freshwater to wells and riparian areas. This may be the case for the Lost River and in other areas where cottonwood groves exist on the east side of the monument.

Wells

Wells are generally used to withdraw water from aquifers. Sufficiently large withdrawals can change directions of groundwater flow. Groundwater withdrawn from an aquifer does not exit the aquifer at natural discharge areas. Information on well locations, groundwater withdrawals, and groundwater levels are needed to properly manage resources dependent upon hydrologic processes.

Monitoring wells within the monument can be used to monitor the level of the shallow aquifer and for contamination. Water levels will reflect the sum total of climatic factors, including precipitation and evapotranspiration. Water samples for these wells can also be tested for hazardous chemicals. Table 4 provides a summary of monitoring wells within WHSA.

Water supply wells for communities outside the monument are found in the Douglas, Boles, San Andres and Snake Tank Road well fields (Huff, 1996, Livingston Associates and John Shomaker and Associates, 2002). The highest concentration of water supply wells in the Tularosa Basin occurs on the eastern margin on alluvial fans where water quality is acceptable. Water level declines associated with the municipal water supply have been modeled by the U. S. Geologic Survey and results indicate the water level declines would probably be limited to areas adjacent to the well fields. The model did not include discharge or withdrawal data from wells toward the center of the basin.

Table 4. Monitoring wells within WHSA and water levels at the time of construction (Barud-Zubillaga, 2000).

Well ID	Northing	Easting	Total Depth (ft)	Depth to Water (top of casing) (ft)	Date of Water Level Measurement
MW-001	32°49"23"	106°16"05"	25	3.58	July 21, 1997
MW-002	32°48"53"	106°15"02"	30	4.125	July 21, 1997
MW-003	32°47"12"	106°10"57"	40	18.0	July 22, 1997
MW-004	32°46"45"	106°10"26"	37	10.4	July 22, 1997
MW-005	32°46"18"	106°10"52"	29	9.4	July 22, 1997
MW-006	32°48"50"	106°15"29"	29.5	3.1	July 23, 1997

Water Quality

The pollution of natural waters can impair the natural function of aquatic and terrestrial ecosystems and negatively impact visitor experience. According to NPS Management Policies, the NPS will determine the quality of WHSA water resources and avoid, whenever possible, the pollution of monument water by human activities occurring within and outside monument boundaries (National Park Service, 2006).

Within WHSA, natural water quality conditions should be maintained "unimpaired" under the National Park Service Organic Act (1916, 16 USC11). Water quality standards relative to WHSA are guided by the Clean Water Act as promulgated by the State of New Mexico. The 2008-2010 State of New Mexico CWA § 303(d)/§ 305(b) Integrated Report does not list any designated use waters within WHSA.

Water resource status and trends are summarized for all parks within the Chihuahuan Desert Inventory and Monitoring Network (Porter et al., 2009). Water quality in WHSA is overwhelmingly controlled by the high rate of evaporation in the basin (60-80 in/yr.) which concentrates the dissolved minerals in the water to > 65,000 mg/L TDS in some areas of the Tularosa Basin. This phenomenon is a common feature of closed basins within the southwestern United States.

Saline and brine groundwater are found throughout the basin with concentrations being higher toward the center of the basin (Figure 13). Fresh water supplies (<1,000 mg/L TDS) are found beneath the alluvial fans at the basin edges and within coarse grain lenses that carry water to the basin center without contact with gypsiferous sediments. Water quality is dominated by calcium, sodium and sulfate.

Concentrations of chloride and sulfate from Lake Lucero samples exceeded USEPA drinking water and freshwater criteria. The highest concentrations of chloride and sulfate (126,000 mg/L and 39,000 respectively) were reported for Lake Lucero in April 1993. Elevated concentrations of metals were reported (National Park Service, 1997).

Data for the headwaters segment of the Lost River were limited to concentrations of metals in streambed sediments and lists of macro invertebrates and diatoms from studies by the New Mexico Environment Department in 1993 (Porter et al, 2009).

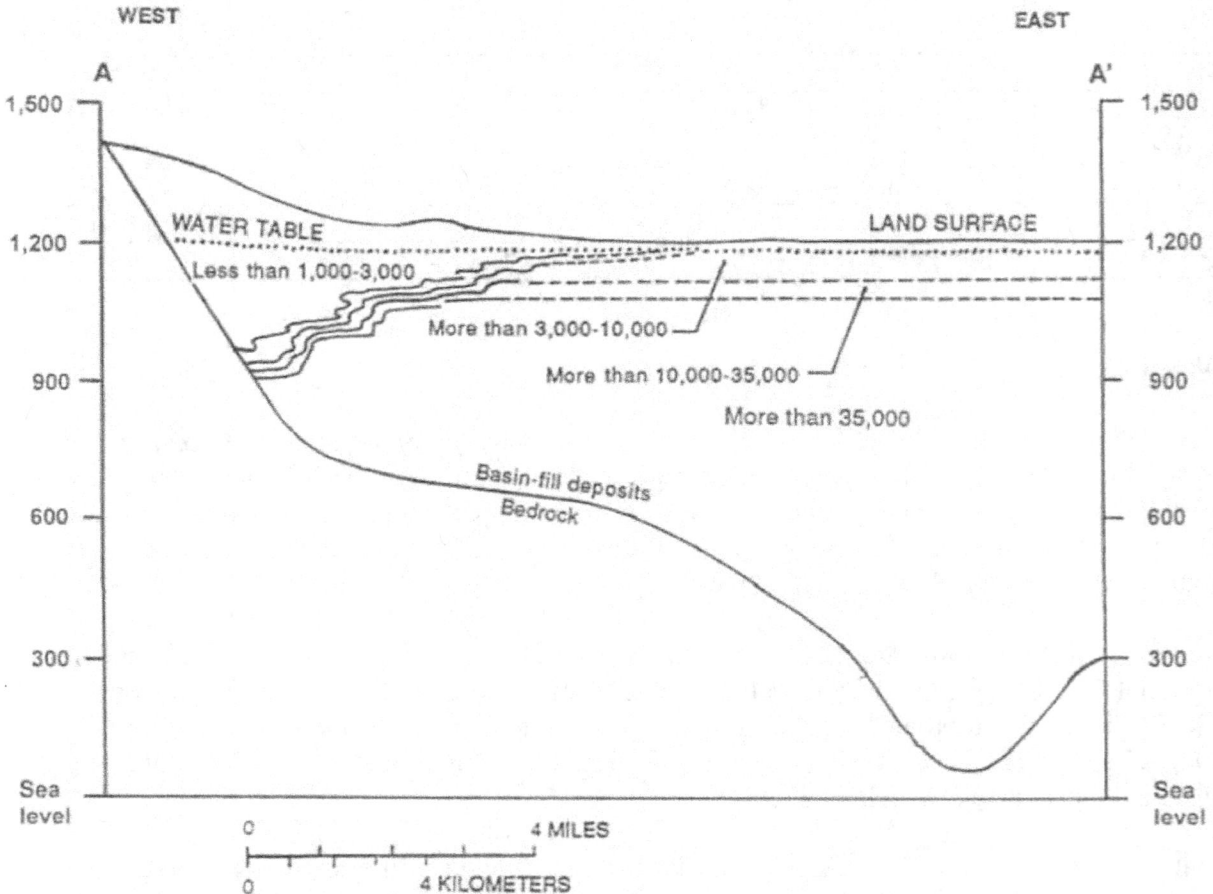

Figure 13. Concentrations of total dissolved solids in groundwater across the Tularosa Basin (Barud-Zubillaga, 2000).

Flora and Fauna

Flora

WHSA is located at the northern limits of the Chihuahan Desert, and as expected, the majority of plants are drought tolerant. In addition, many of these plants must be adapted to alkaline, nutrient poor soils with high gypsum content. The highly mineralized water table under these soils ranges from about 3 feet below the surface at Lake Lucero and the interdune flats to more than 20 feet outside the dune field.

Plants surviving here must also endure being buried by moving dunes and be able to tolerate extreme fluctuations in temperature, with common sub-freezing winter lows to occasional 100+ summer days.

28

The majority of plants in WHSA are found in 6 distinct ecological units -- A through F--, primarily on the basis of soil type and mineral concentration, dune activity, and water availability. A description of each unit from http://www.ohranger.com/white-sands/plants, along with examples of plant species found in each, follows:

Lake Lucero (Unit A) and Alkali Flat (Unit B) - Alkali Flat is the exposed lake bed of ancient Pleistocene Lake Otero, which has dried into its present condition. Occasionally water pools in the southern end of the flat, forming seasonal Lake Lucero. Extreme alkaline conditions and occasional flooding prevent the growth of plant life in these two areas except for a few scattered grasses and pickleweed. Saltcedar, an exotic invasive shrub, has managed to survive in places along the fringes of these two areas.

Unit C is primarily dome, transverse, and barchan dunes and represents some of the most extreme environmental conditions for plant life on the monument. These dunes creep forward as much as 30 feet per year and even fast-growing plants such as yucca and rosemary mint cannot outgrow them. Occasional pedestals topped with sumac, rosemary mint, or saltcedar are left in the trail of a moving dune. The interdune areas may contain sand verbena, evening primrose, woolly paper flower, Indian rice grass, yucca, ephedra, and alkali sacaton.

Unit D is composed mostly of parabolic dunes, which extend two to three miles into the dunefield from its southern and eastern boundaries. These are slower moving, vegetated-dunes and are separated by large grassy, interdune areas. Grasses found here include several members of the dropseed tribe, gypsum grama, little bluestem, sandhill muhly, and alkali sacaton. Soaptree yucca, rosemary mint, skunkbush sumac, Rio Grande cottonwood, and scattered stands of the exotic saltcedar are the primary woody plants found in this area. This area has the most complex and varied plant community on the monument.

Unit E can best be described as a saltbush/alkali sacaton association, dotted with an occasional sumac bush, hedgehog cactus and cane cholla. This extremely flat area of grey-green vegetation over gypsum/alkali soils extends from the eastern and southern monument boundaries to the edges of the dunefield.

Unit F is composed of mesquite hummocks near the edges of Alkali Flat and Lake Lucero and creosote bush on alluvial fans that extend to the monument boundary from the base of the San Andres Mountains. Alkali sacaton and a few other grasses are found above the lake floodplain into the margins of the mesquite dunes (composed of quartz sand rather than gypsum).

Fauna

Forty-four species of mammals, twenty-six species of reptiles, six species of amphibians and nearly 100 families of insects have been recorded within White Sands National Monument. Most animals inhabit the margins of the dune field and the adjacent desert plain.

As in other deserts, most animals that live here are nocturnal. In order to conserve water and avoid extreme heat, many desert animals stay underground during the day, emerging from their burrows after sunset to search for food. Evidence of their activities can be found in the sand the next morning. The Big Dune Nature Trail is a good place to search for animal tracks and sign.

Even at night, dark animals are easily spotted against the white background of the gypsum sand, making them easy victims for predators. Some small animals, including the Apache pocket mouse, the Bleached Earless Lizard, the Cowles Prairie Lizard, and numerous insects, have evolved a white coloration that camouflages them in the dunes.

Animals are rarely seen within the center of the dune field. The extreme temperatures and the lack of food, shelter and standing water combine to restrict their number. But they are here, even in the heart of the dunes. Like plants, most animals are found in the interdune flats. During the day, watch for darkling beetles, lizards and birds venturing onto the sand. At night, pocket mice and kangaroo rats forage for seeds, and kit fox hunt the mice and rats.

The oryx, or gemsbok, is a large (450 pounds) African antelope that now lives in southern New Mexico. Oryx were introduced onto the White Sands Missile Range by the state of New Mexico to establish a huntable big game population. Oryx have successfully adapted to the area and have spread throughout the Tularosa Basin, including White Sands National Monument. The National Park Service considers the oryx to be a threat to the monument's native plants and animals and has fenced the monument boundary to exclude the oryx.

Aquatic fauna are adapted to the saline environments. A list of macroinvertebrates and diatoms from Lost River is available for samples collected in 1993 by the New Mexico Environment Department (Porter et al., 2009). Macroinvertebrate taxa richness was 7, dominated by *Trichochoiza* sp., a salt tolerant water bug. The diatom community consisted of halophilic species found typically in coastal estuaries. The rare White Sands Pupfish, the only fish native to the Tularosa Basin, can be found in Lost River, a stream that originates in the Sacramento Mountains. Lost River enters the eastern part of the dune field and flows about two miles before disappearing in the sand.

Air Quality

Under the Clean Air Act (42 USC 7401-7671q, as amended in 1990), park managers have a responsibility to protect air quality and related values from the adverse effects of air pollution. Protection of air quality in national parks requires knowledge of the origin, transport, and fate of air pollution, as well as its impacts on resources. Air quality was identified as a potential vital sign for the network because of its importance as both an anthropogenic and natural driver of change (Reiser et al. 2008).

WHSA is a Class II area. Class II areas of the country are protected under the Clean Air Act, but have less stringent protection from air pollution damage than a Class I area, except in specified cases.

Fundamental Geologic and Water Resources and Values

It is important for WHSA to identify the resources and values critical to achieving the monument's purpose and maintaining its significance. The reasons for identifying fundamental and other important resources and values are:

1. To define and understand the most important resources and values that support the monument's purpose and significance. If these resources and values are degraded or eliminated, they then jeopardize the monument's purpose and significance.
2. To ensure that the planning team and public understand the key elements that sustains the monument's purpose and significance.
3. To help planning and management activities focus on larger issues and concerns regarding protection of the resources and values that support the monument's purpose and significance.
4. To allow the planning team to test alternatives and estimate how each might influence the fundamental and important resources and values of the monument.
5. To become the building blocks in creating a future vision and management strategy for the monument.

Identifying the fundamental and important resources and values at WHSA helps ensure that all planning is focused on what is most significant about the monument. As presented earlier in this report, it is recommended that both geologic and water resources be defined as *fundamental resources* at WHSA, receiving the highest level of protection.

The following sections follow a format currently used by the NPS Denver Service Center (DSC) Planning Division in preparing a park-specific *Foundation Document*. This includes the following six questions that are answered for *fundamental resources* (geologic and water resources) at the monument:

1. What is the importance of geologic and water resources?
2. What is the adequacy of the existing geologic and water resources information?
3. What are the current conditions and related trends of the geologic and water resources?
4. What are the current and potential threats to the geologic and water resources?
5. Who are the stakeholders who have an interest in WHSA's geologic and water resources?
6. Which laws and policies apply to geologic and water resources at the monument?

These questions are answered from interviews and existing technical references provided to the authors.

What is the importance of geologic and water resources?

Geologic Resources

WHSA contains the world's largest gypsum dune field and the preservation of it and related natural resources is the basis of the enabling legislation for WHSA. Wind, water and sediment supply play a central role in the dynamics of the dune field. Since these factors are not bound by monument borders, management staff should look beyond the monument boundary when making important decisions and long-term plans.

During the 2003 Geoindicators meeting, participants prioritized the most important geologic and hydrologic features and processes at White Sands National Monument as:

- Dune features and processes, including dune formation and reactivation, groundwater chemistry and groundwater levels.
- Lacustrine features and processes, including lake levels and salinity.

The principle features and processes of dunes remain a subject of research (KellerLynn, 2008). Groundwater levels and their capacity to support vegetation play an important role in dune dynamics (KellerLynn, 2008). As the groundwater levels decline, dune-anchoring vegetation diminishes, causing dune movement. Conversely, as groundwater levels rise and support more plants, dunes stabilize.

Dunefields

Shifting or migrating dunes alter drainage patterns creating new pathways for water to enter the monument and in some cases create barriers to water flow. Since 2003, new drainages into the monument are known to have resulted in the introduction of the pupfish—a state-listed threatened species—to the monument (KellerLynn, 2008).

Soil Crusts

Soil crusts are important resources at WHSA as indicators of ecosystem stability, health, and climate change. Soil crusts come in two forms, biological and physical. Biological crusts occupy an intermediate ecological position between active dunes and vegetated surfaces in the monument. They are critical to plant growth because they fix nitrogen into the system and bind soil. Physical crusts are inorganic and caused by features such as platy soil surface particles, an accumulation of salt, or, as rainfall drives finer grains into pore spaces, a decrease in pore space (Rosentreter et al., 2007). Both physical and biological crusts are important soil binders.

The importance and hydroecological role of a soil crust is very much site dependent.

Physical crusts can only occur on soil with a large distribution of grain size and by definition have decreased pore space. Therefore the formation of a physical crust will lead to a decrease in infiltration and an increase in runoff. Low infiltration can impact vegetation communities by preventing rainfall from reaching root zones. Increased runoff can increase the potential for erosion. Areas where vegetative cover has been removed are vulnerable to physical crust formation.

Biological soil crusts can impact water infiltration in unexpected ways. On silty soils a biological crust can prevent the formation of a physical crust and so increase infiltration and decrease runoff. On silty soils a biological crust means a deeper wetting front during rain storms and a wetter root zone. On sandy soils, where more porosity means higher infiltration rates, a biological crust can decrease infiltration by covering the sandy soil with a biological mat with lower porosity. A decrease in infiltration will mean an increase in runoff. Both of these attributes are important for the dune ecosystem.

Unique Features

Yardangs

White Sands has been identified as a premier U.S. site for yardangs. The variety at White Sands is great (Steven Fryberger, in KellerLynn, 2008). Unfortunately, most visitors never see these features because the best examples are not accessible. Yet they are worth noting as an important geomorphic feature of White Sands because the monument may contain the world's best examples of these features. Figure 14 shows a typical yardang at White Sands.

Yardangs occur in arid environments where wind is a significant erosional force (Fryberger, 2001). The widespread occurrence of yardangs within the barchan dune areas of WHSA suggests a long history of wind erosion at the monument. These intriguing features not only offer interpretative value, study of them may lead to a better understanding of desert erosional processes.

There may also be a connection between the development of plant pedestals and yardangs. Fryberger, 2001, suggests that as vegetation on a plant pedestal dies, it will take the form of a yardang. Since yardangs represent a more significant wind regime, their location, orientation, size and age, in conjunction with plant pedestals, may record wind erosion history at large and small scales.

Additionally, since yardangs occur extensively on Mars (McCauley, 1973), they are of interest to planetary scientists.

Additional photographs and information may be found on the internet at http://www2.nature.nps.gov/geology/parks/whsa/geows/Chapter8.htm#sec5.

Figure 14. Photo of a large yardang at White Sands National Monument. Prevailing wind in this photo is from the left foreground to the right background (southwest to northeast) (Fryberger, 2001).

Pedestals

There are two types of pedestals that occur in White Sands National Monument: plant and crystal. Plant pedestals are often a sign of severe wind or sheet wash erosion (Pellant et al., 2000). In WHSA, several competing theories describe plant pedestal formation. One theory is that the pedestals are remnants of older dunes that have largely weathered away. It is thought that deep-rooted plants are able to survive longer while surrounding vegetation dies off perhaps due to a drop in the water table. The deep roots preserve parts of a dune and form a pedestal. Another theory with a cultural connection is that the tops of the preexisting dune had been used as campsites and campfires ossified the gypsum sand, effectively creating a resistant cap which impedes erosion. Plant pedestals are known to provide habit for a variety of organisms. As "island" communities, these pedestals demonstrate an important relationship between geological and biological processes.

Crystal pedestals are an intriguing feature of the landscape at White Sands occurring on Alkali Flat in and out of the monument. Figure 15 shows the area of the monument known to include crystal pedestals. The pedestals are essentially accumulations of coarse gypsum cleavage fragments and crystals (Love, personal communication, 2008) and are not related to vegetation. Crystals found in the pedestals generally appear to be aligned in at least two directions (Figure 16).

There remains uncertainty as to the origin of these crystal pedestals. One theory is that the pedestals grew upward along with groundwater upwelling through playa lake beds. Another proposed mechanism is that the pedestals are gypsum crystals that fell in cracks, perhaps formed via earthquake or erosion (soil piping) in lake beds (Love, personal communication, 2008). Similar crystal pedestals have been observed on Mars making White Sands an important location for planetary research. The gypsum crystals are cemented together by capillary water and a fluctuating water table and are exposed as the lake bed erodes.

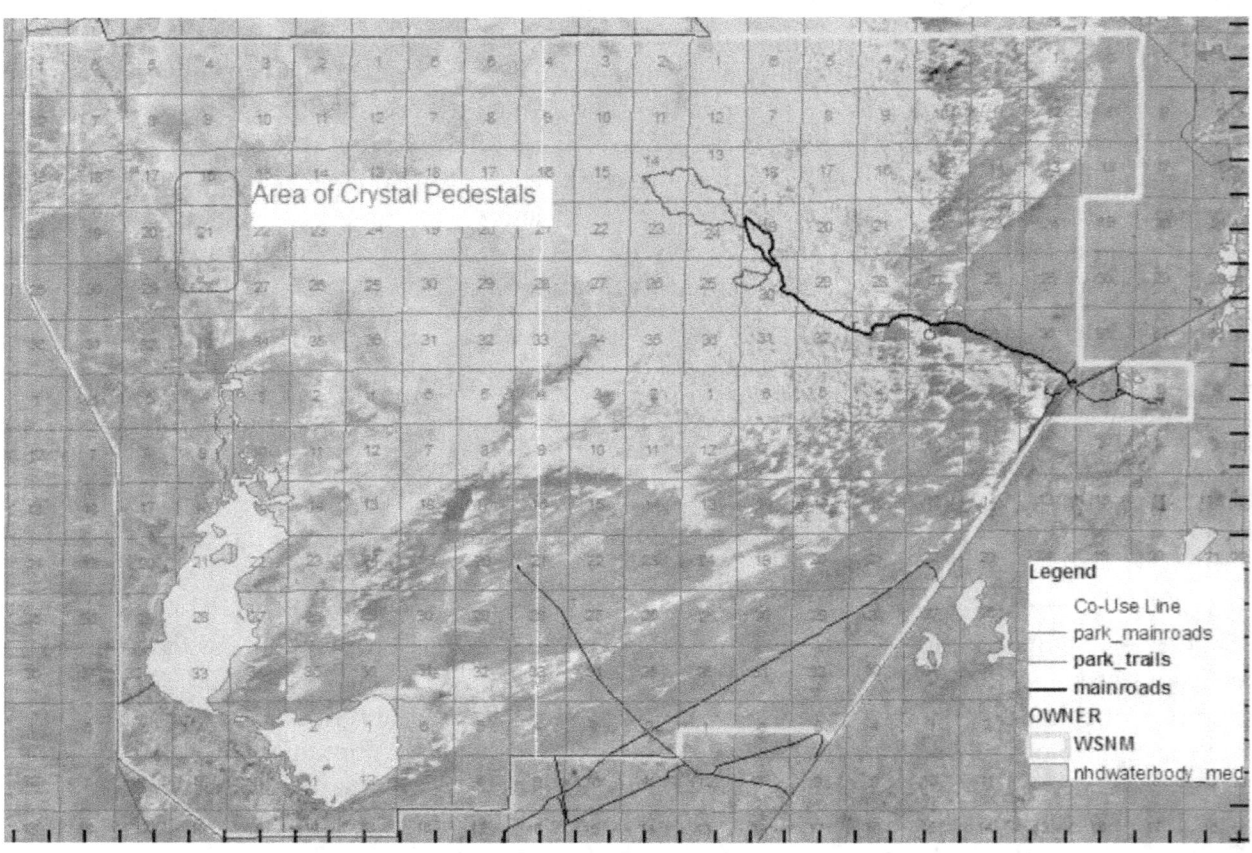

Figure 15. Locations of crystal monuments at White Sands National Monument. Crystal pedestals have been observed in the northwest portion of the monument as well as in other parts of the Alkali Flat outside the monument (Source: White Sands National Monument).

Figure 16. Photo of crystal pedestals of White Sands National Monument. The mechanisms for the formation of these pedestals is poorly understood and the subject of current research (Photograph by Dave Love, New Mexico Bureau of Geology and Mineral Resources).

Interdunes

Interdunes provide important habitat for much of the flora and fauna of White Sands. The evolution of interdunes is, obviously, tied to that of dunes but since the interdunes host a greater and more abundant variety of species, interdune evolution determines species growth and distribution.

Interdunes are sites for sediment preservation since they are commonly overridden by moving dunes, increasing chances for preservation in the sediment record. Because of their preservation potential, they are of great interest to geologists studying sediments and rocks for what they may reveal about environmental conditions at the time of deposition. Since sediments are well preserved in interdunes, trenches dug in them can reveal historical snapshots and allow scientists to construct a history of dune movement (Fryberger, 2001).

Bajadas

Coalesced alluvial fans on the west side of the monument distribute water, have distinct plant communities and soil types, and are thought to be the primary source of groundwater recharge for the basin underlying the monument. Bajadas form when alluvial fans converge. The resulting apron of sediment is called a bajada. These deposits consist of gravels and sands and interfinger with the finer evaporite and lacustrine deposits of the basin center (Orr and Myers, 1986).

Paleontology

Fossil mammoth tracks and microinvertebrate fossils from Lake Otero sediments occur within the monument (Bruce Allen, in KellerLynn, 2008). Such fossils are indicators of past climate and may contain a record of conditions during the Pleistocene.

Several sets of late Pleistocene mammoth tracks preserved in convex relief in a soft gypsum matrix have been found in the monument. Radiocarbon dating (^{14}C) of the track-bearing sediments suggests that the tracks are at least 30,000 yrs old (Lucas et al., 2007). These trace fossils are considered extremely delicate and subject to erosion. Since May 2007, monument staff has discovered more than ten sets of mammoth tracks throughout the monument without making a concerted effort to systematically inventory the fossil tracks. This suggests that a rigorous survey may yield additional sets of tracks.

Lake Sediments

Lake Otero sediments in the monument represent the latest part of the lake history and hold clues to dune processes, habitat for early humans and regional geologic history, including, possibly, a record of micrometeorite falls that may have affected mammoth and bison populations (Dave Love in KellerLynn, 2008).

Extraterrestrial Research

An intriguing aspect of White Sands is its recognized similarity to Mars and the Moon. The NASA rover, Opportunity, landed on Mars on January 24, 2004 in a large playa which bears striking similarities to the Alkali Flat. Research has shown that dunes on Mars were formed by wind and past water erosion in a playa system similar to White Sands. Data have shown that the dunes of Mars are also made up of gypsum, thus research of the White Sands dunes may reveal information about processes and conditions on Mars.

Other features including crystal pedestals and smaller-scale surface formations such as "fins" observed on Mars also occur in the monument (Figure 17). The "fins" are cemented gypsum sand grains and crack-filling gypsum cement along fissures in older sand dune deposits (Love, personal communication, 2009).

Figure 17. Photo comparison of fins on Mars and at White Sands National Monument. Fins observed on Mars (left) may have formed under conditions similar to fins seen at White Sands (right). Source: NASA/Jet Propulsion Laboratory and White Sands National Monument.

The major focus of Mars related research at White Sands is based around three questions:

1. What influence does the atmosphere have on gypsum soils of White Sands and Mars?
2. How is gypsum formed, concentrated and broken down to form the dune fields of White Sands and Mars?
3. How do dunes at White Sands and Mars develop and migrate?

Teams from the University of California at Davis; Indiana University; and University of Texas at Austin are currently pursuing these lines of research. The University of Texas team has been creating highly accurate three dimensional maps of the monument's dunes and playa system for several consecutive years. These data and maps may be useful for planning and management as well as Inventory and Monitoring Program objectives.

Species Adaptations to Geology

The geologic characteristics of WHSA have become central to the adaptations of several plant and animal species. For example, the shifting sands are believed to drive the soaptree yucca's ability to grow upward to a foot a year to keep its leaves above the sand. Also, in some cases, species have adapted to the color of the sand. The bleached earless lizard, as well as a variety of insect species that occur in the monument, have adapted to match the color of the white sands. These species adaptations are tangible and fascinating examples of the effects of geology on endemism.

Water Resources

Few perennial water sources (springs, wetlands, perennial streams) exist in or near the monument. The occurrence of water and its quantity and quality directly impact dune stability. Permanent and migratory wildlife depend on the water and riparian community associated with area water sources. These water sources probably host metapopulations of endemic species.

Based on the 2006 NPS Management Policies for water resources (National Park Service, 2006):

- WHSA will avoid the pollution of water by human activities occurring within and outside the monument.
- WHSA will manage watersheds as complete hydrologic systems, and minimize human disturbance to the natural upland processes that deliver water, sediment, and dissolved solids.
- WHSA will manage wetlands in compliance with NPS mandates and requirements of Executive Order 11990 (Wetland Protection), the Clean Water Act, the Rivers and Harbors Appropriation Act of 1899, and the procedures described in Director's Order Orders 77-1. The service will 1) provide leadership and take action to prevent the destruction, loss, and degradation of wetlands; 2) preserve and enhance the natural and beneficial value of wetlands; and 3) avoid direct and indirect support of new construction in wetlands unless there are not practicable alternatives and the proposed action includes all practicable measures to minimize harm to wetlands. The NPS will implement a "no net loss" of wetlands property.
- WHSA will 1) manage for the preservation of floodplain values; 2) minimize potentially hazardous conditions associated with flooding; and 3) comply with the NPS Organic Act and all other federal laws and executive orders related to the management of activities in flood-prone area including Executive Order 11988 (Floodplain Management), NEPA, applicable provision of the Clean Water Act, and the Rivers and Harbors Act of 1899.

Surface Water

Lost River

Perennial flow in the Lost River exists only on DOD property at the northwest corner of the monument and supports an adapted aquatic ecosystem and is critical to species protection.

The flow is lost to infiltration and evaporation and may sustain dune stability and groundwater levels underneath the dunes. Thus water in perennial streams east of the monument is important to White Sands National Monument.

Lake Lucero

Lake Lucero is a unique and important hydrologic feature. Anecdotal reports by monument staff of visitor use suggest it is the second most visited fundamental resource in the monument along with the dune field. In wet times it is a recharge area while in dry times it is a groundwater discharge area. The regional groundwater gradient is toward the lake and continually brings hypersaline groundwater to the playa which evaporates and leaves behind mineral precipitates. Surface water transports very little gypsum to the playa and contributes very little to the formation of the dunes (Allmendinger and Titus, 1973). Surface water occasionally fills the lake and supports migrating bird populations. Ponded water dissolves the upper crust of the playa, causing the salinity of the surface water to increase. However, this process is not important for gypsum sand formation. Whether wet or dry, Lake Lucero contributes greatly to the biodiversity of the area.

Groundwater

As a major controlling factor of dune activity and dune biodiversity, it is important to monitor groundwater levels and the quality of groundwater. Water levels within two to three feet of ground surface support vegetation that stabilizes dunes. During wet times, interdune areas of sand erosion can become saturated with shallow pools preventing wind erosion. The wet-dry cycle of the interdunes can dissolve and re-precipitate minerals creating a physical crust that is more resistant to wind erosion. By preventing erosion of the interdune, these wet periods exert important geomorphic control by decreasing dune movement.

Wetlands occupy low lying areas and seasonally impound surface water. Wetlands support both endemic and migratory animals.

The ecological community adapted to the dune field and surrounding area is dependent on the high groundwater level. The unsaturated zone, that area between the ground surface and the water table, is important for a process known as "capillary action". The process pulls water up and makes it available for plants, burrowing animals and soil forming processes. A long-term (50 year plus) rise or fall of the water table of only a few feet would initiate major changes in dune dynamics at the monument. In contrast with Great Sand Dunes National Park where a number of other factors affect dune dynamics, groundwater level plays a primary role in dunefield growth, erosion and movement at White Sands.

Water Chemistry

Groundwater transports a large quantity of gypsum to Lake Lucero (Allmendinger and Titus, 1973). The dissolution of Permian evaporates in the Yeso Formation and lacustrine deposits provide the necessary minerals for gypsum and selenite formation. As groundwater evaporates from the surface of Lake Lucero, selenite crystals grow. These crystals are eventually abraded by wind and provide the source of the sand for the dunes (Allmendinger and Titus, 1973). Recent research, however, calls into question the importance of this process in adding gypsum grains to the dunefield (Fryberger, 2001).

The quality of surface water and groundwater contributes to a unique assemblage of plants and animals that are adapted to saline environments. Groundwater chemistry controls vegetation and thus affects dune stability. Increased salinity will result in greater dune activity as anchoring vegetation dies off (KellerLynn, 2003). Water quality drives the ecohydrologic function of the landscape in and around WHSA and thus the quality of surface water and groundwater is important at WHSA.

What is the adequacy of existing geologic and water resource information?

Geologic Resources

Dune Processes

Current research by Anna Szynkiewicz, Gary Kocurek, and Rip Langford is refining the understanding of the origin and timing of dune formation, dune dynamics, and the interactions between eolian deflation of dunes and playa lakes (KellerLynn, 2008). The Heart of Sands quadrangle (Figure 18), Kocurek's study area, includes all dune types. Kocurek and Langford are writing a monitoring protocol for dune dynamics, and Langford and Szynkiewicz are creating conceptual models for the gypsum sand dunes at White Sands National Monument and Guadalupe Mountains National Park. Kocurek and colleagues have baseline LiDAR data acquired in 2007.

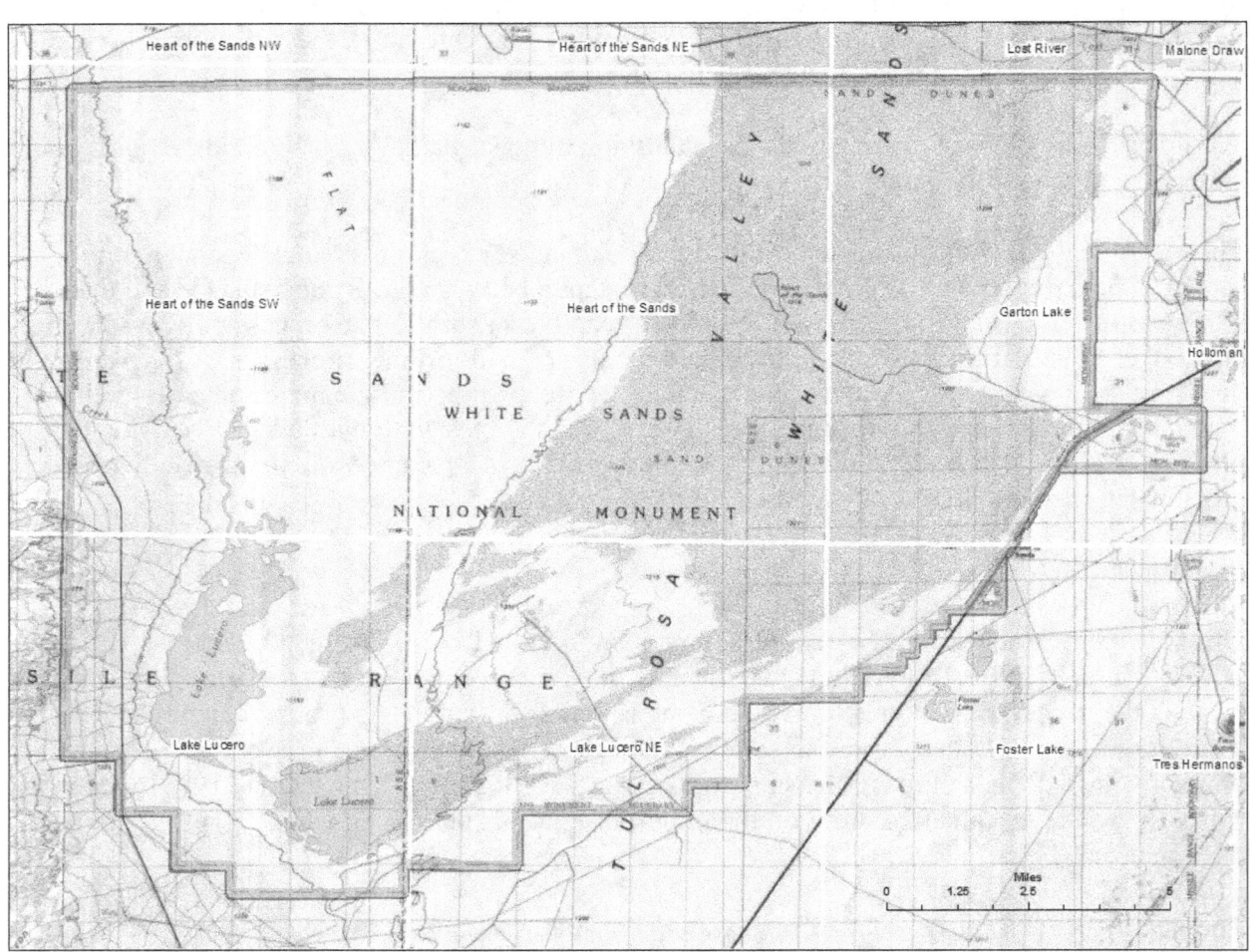

Figure 18. USGS 7.5 minute quads comprising White Sands National Monument.

Additional study of the relationship between dunes and groundwater is needed (KellerLynn, 2008). While it's generally understood that a lower water table results in greater dune activity, the following mechanisms are not well understood:

- Dune stability – specifically as related to the unsaturated zone
- Gypsum production
- Dune formation as it is related to groundwater

Research in these processes may allow for a better understanding of the interrelationship of dune and hydrogeologic processes. Management of the dune resources will likely benefit from a greater knowledge of the effects of groundwater dynamics on dune processes.

During the Geoindicators meeting in 2003, participants suggested that a map identifying the various generations of dunes, ranging from active dunes to the oldest fossil dunes, would be useful for resource management. Figures 4 and 10 provide some information on the extent of the active and inactive dunefields but do not focus on dune dynamics. A map with color classifications of dune activity would provide an important context for resource management and monument operations. Such a map would likely require regularly scheduled revisions as new data are collected. A time-synched map series such as this would give managers an understanding of dynamic dune processes and may help identify how management actions affect those processes. This in turn will guide management decisions to best preserve the dune resources. It is generally agreed that Seager et al. (1987), Figure 5, should serve as the basic digital geologic map for White Sands National Monument (KellerLynn, 2008).

The Department of Defense at White Sands Missile Range has acquired and interpreted satellite imagery of the dune field, playa lakes, and surrounding areas. These data (shapefiles) could likely be shared with the National Park Service if a representative from White Sands National Monument requested them.

A comprehensive bibliography of dune research, including a catalog of existing data and imagery, should be compiled (KellerLynn, 2003). The 2002 New Mexico Geological Society publication titled "Geology of White Sands" currently represents the best available, published compilation for geology of the southern Tularosa Basin. The National Park Service maintains a website containing links to online resources for southern Tularosa Basin geology at http://www.nps.gov/archive/whsa/home.htm.

Paleontology

Even though a literature review summarizing the paleontological resources in the monument was completed in 2007 (National Park Service, 2007), a detailed inventory of paleontological resources in the monument is still needed (KellerLynn, 2008). As noted earlier, several sets of mammoth tracks have been discovered since 2007 by monument staff. Such discoveries suggest that a more rigorous inventory would result in of the discovery of additional sites. Paleontological resources are summarized in the NPS Chihuahuan Desert Network (CHDN) inventory and monitoring report (National Park Service, 2007). The section for the CHDN is included as Appendix A.

Key findings from the CHDN Paleontological Inventory:
- Paleontological discoveries are documented from an area adjacent to the monument boundary. There is limited potential for future discovery of fossils at WHSA.
- Pleistocene mammalian track-ways have been documented on the nearby White Sands Missile Range.

While the CHDN report noted a low potential for new fossil discoveries, documented finds adjacent to the monument may suggest otherwise. The CHDN report also did not address microfossils, which may occur in abundance in the monument and may represent an important resource for further study.

Mammoth tracks observed in the monument have not been adequately dated with radiocarbon methods. Dating of the lake bed sediments via radiocarbon techniques will help constrain the age of the tracks (KellerLynn, 2008).

A plethora of microfossils likely exist in Lake Otero sediments (KellerLynn, 2003). Since these fossils are indicators of past climate, it would be valuable to the monument to analyze the sediments in order to model paleoecological conditions. Security measures in place in the White Sands Missile Range have prevented thorough study of Lake Otero sediments. Extensive study in other regional lakes reveals a wealth of paleontological information (KellerLynn, 2008).

Soils and Sediments

The scale at which the existing soils map (Neher and Bailey, 1976) was produced is not useful for making management decisions (KellerLynn, 2008) and should be remapped to at least the national map standard of 1:24,000. Mapping should include physical and biological soil crusts. As of May 2008, the Natural Resource Conservation Service (NRCS) was in the process of updating the soils map of the Tularosa Basin (Dave Love, New Mexico Bureau of Geology and Mineral Resources, written communication, May 16, 2008).

The digital geologic map produced by the GRI Program (based on Seager et al., 1987) does not include soils. Monument staff can contact Pete Biggam, NPS' Soils Program Manager in the Geologic Resources Division (pete_biggam@nps.gov or 303-987-6948) for assistance with their soils mapping and soil resource management needs.

Bruce Allen, Bob Myers and Dave Love are working on a report of their investigations in the Tularosa Basin. The work is located mostly north and west of the monument and focuses primarily in Quaternary spring, marsh and lake deposits. The report will include radiocarbon dates for sediments from these deposits (Dave Love, New Mexico Bureau of Geology and Mineral Resources, written communication, August, 2008).

Further study of sediment sequences and composition is needed to better understand ecosystem change and human influences on the ecosystem (KellerLynn, 2008). Sediment processes record environmental conditions at the time of deposition and therefore provides a context for further study as well as monument management decisions. Analysis of sediment cores from Lake Lucero would likely lead to a better understanding of how Lake Lucero developed over time.

In addition, if eolian sediments from the dunes could be dated, the ages of different portions of the dunefield could be better understood and tied to events in the history of the ancient lakes, evaporite flats and playas. Sediment processes associated with flooding of Lake Lucero and the degree to which sediments from these events contribute to dune formation is poorly understood (Fryberger, 2001).

Biological Soil Crusts

Reports and data on biological soil crusts should be compiled and made available to NPS staff. Sources for information on biological soil crusts include (KellerLynn, 2008):

- Data from vegetation plots in White Sands Missile Range
- Data from Holloman Air Force Base
- Data from a study of ATV tracks in 2000 and 2002 in the monument
- AVIRIS imagery from University of Texas–El Paso.

Additional study of soil crust resilience, recovery rates and the areal extent of different biological soil crusts occurring in the monument is also needed (KellerLynn, 2008).

Yardangs

While it is generally understood that yardangs occur in the barchanoid dune fields of WHSA (Fryberger, 2001), an inventory of locations, orientations, and other characteristics including size, shape and degree of weathering would inform our understanding of the erosional history of the monument. There are a number of questions concerning yardangs such as:

1. Does the occurrence of yardangs correlate spatially with areas of little gypsum sand deposition?
2. What is the developmental relationship between yardangs and plant pedestals?
3. How well do yardangs represent similarly shaped features on Mars?
4. What do yardangs tell us about the history of wind erosion at WHSA?
5. Are existing yardangs eroding and where might yardangs form in the future?

A thorough inventory of yardangs will provide baseline data for research focused on answering these questions.

Water Resources

The existing water-related information for WHSA consists of studies and monitoring efforts by NPS staff and other agencies that range from a single sampling event to multi-year monitoring programs. For example, water levels are monitored in the monument's observation wells. In addition, the Chihuahuan Desert Inventory and Monitoring Network has produced several reports, the most recent a summary of relevant information available (Porter et al, 2009). However, much of the data needed for the development of a conceptual model that relates the Jarilla Fault to surface and groundwater flow, and overall ecohydrologic function of natural resources at WHSA is not readily available.

The following is a summary of historic and current efforts to collect water resources information at WHSA.

Surface Water

A thorough inventory of wetlands and surface water features has not been performed and is therefore needed (KellerLynn, 2003). Some information is available on water levels and water quality for Lake Lucero but has not been pulled together for analysis and interpretation. A nine-year study on wetlands on adjacent DOD property is available (Martin et al., 2004). This study focuses on overall importance of wetlands, habitat availability, species composition, wildlife utilization, and the occurrence of exotic invaders. It does not illustrate the role of geology in maintaining these features. This study should be considered before any inventory of wetlands and surface water sources in WHSA.

Dr. Elizabeth Walsh, University of Texas at El Paso is working on the systematics and ecology of aquatic macroinvertebrates of the Chihuahuan Desert. In 2007-2008, her team sampled a variety of aquatic habitats including Lake Lucero, interdunal areas that were flooded, a stock tank, a spring, the Lost River, and several locations adjacent to the monument. These efforts included water chemistry and zooplankton surveys. The State of New Mexico has also surveyed the Lost River for aquatic invertebrates (Bustos, personal communication, 2009). No detailed report is available.

Two reported investigations on water contamination were available for this report. In 1998, the USGS analyzed water samples from two wells (MW2 and MW3) and the Lost River for contaminants entering the monument from HAFB. Very small concentrations were found but were below detectable limits and below allowable maximum contaminant levels. In 2003, six solid leaf samples from the Lost River were analyzed by the USGS for perchlorate. All samples had concentrations below detectable limits.

Groundwater

Proximity to DOD activities that utilize hazardous materials has raised concerns in the past concerning groundwater contamination. Thus, several groundwater quality studies have been performed both inside and outside the monument. The USGS has installed monitoring wells inside the monument (KellerLynn, 2003) which, along with the water quality studies, have resulted in a better understanding of shallow groundwater. No indications of groundwater contamination have been reported (Reid and Reiser, 2005). However, the current configuration of wells is not optimized to detect contaminant plumes entering the monument. Placement should be along the eastern monument boundary and an appropriate sampling depth found through geophysical studies designed to detect highly transmissive zones.

Even though several numerical groundwater flow models are available (Finch, 2006; Huff, 2005), a regional, basin-wide conceptual model of the relationship between groundwater levels, groundwater withdrawals and the eolian ecosystem is lacking. Water users employ groundwater flow models to predict water-level declines and future water-supply shortages. Models for the Tularosa Basin are generally limited to the eastern half and do not include hydrologic conditions west of the Jarilla Fault. However, the City of El Paso has a model to manage groundwater withdrawals from the Hueco Bolson, which is located 60 miles to the south of the monument and is hydraulically connected to the western half of the Tularosa Basin.

The possibility of a perched aquifer occurring beneath the dune field has not been investigated. The relationship between local groundwater gradients and regional groundwater gradients could be better defined. Data from the observation wells near WHSA headquarters and the picnic loop, compared to groundwater data for the Basin-fill aquifer (Huff, 2004) indicate that the local water table is generally eighty feet higher than expected (Porter et al., 2009). Several reports attribute this to a perched water table. Monitoring of water levels and quality in the six existing wells within the monument is needed to provide context for development of ecohydrologic conceptual models. These data would also help illuminate the relationships between regional groundwater flow and water quality, local groundwater flow and water quality, lake levels and water quality, and dune processes. In addition, a new observation well that penetrates the clay layer found in each of the current observation wells, along with expansion of the existing groundwater monitoring well network to better define aquifer characteristics, should be considered.

Another notable data gap concerns the "Garton Well". This was once a flowing artesian well and discharged into a man-made pond that served recreationists. The well no longer flows. Verbal reports from monument staff (Bustos, personal communication, 2009) indicate that there have been efforts to restore flow from the well, including the use of explosives. This well should be put to appropriate use or properly closed.

Other reports from Mr. Bustos indicate the presence of at least three hand-dug wells. During the site visit for this report the team visited one dug well on the west side of Lake Lucero. If the hand-dug wells are not historic features, they should be properly closed.

The effects of surface and groundwater contaminants on selenite formation are unclear. Brines with altered chemistries due to contamination may not produce quality selenite crystals or may produce smaller crystals.

What are the current conditions and related trends of the geologic and water resources?

Geologic Resources

In general, current conditions of geologic resources/features at White Sands are reflected above under **Description of Natural Resources – Geologic Resources**. Current conditions are also described in the following section in the context of threats and issues concerning these resources.

Dunes

Dune processes observed today are driven largely by prevailing northeast winds and while Fryberger, 2001, finds no evidence for older wind regimes, "fossil" dunes found east and south of the main dunefield may offer information about historical wind and climate regimes.

The eolian system appears to be very sensitive to the elevation of the groundwater table (Fryberger, 2001).

It is not clear whether the dune field is growing or shrinking. Origin and timing of dune formation, dune movement, and the interactions between eolian deflation and playa lakes are not well understood and is the subject of current research. A better understanding of these processes may help determine current trends and in changes in the size of the dune field.

Similarly, given the lack of basic inventories for several important geologic resources including fossil mammoth tracks, lake sediment microfossils and yardang distribution and abundance, it is not clear whether or not these resources are currently in a state of decline (erosion) or not. However, Fryberger (2001) in stating the need for more research on yardangs noted that these features are presently undamaged.

Soil Crusts

Soil crusts in White Sands National Monument appear robust, and potential problems are unknown. Crusts in sulfate-rich soils form quickly (within a few years) so that foot-traffic disturbances are less likely to create long-term problems (Love, written communication, 2008).

Water Resources

Surface Water

Neither the National Park Service nor its cooperators have conducted a comprehensive inventory of wetlands within the monument, but anecdotal evidence indicates that wetlands, and thereby wetland species, are disappearing (KellerLynn, 2008). Source areas for basin wetlands have not been investigated and it is therefore difficult to determine why or even if water sources are disappearing. A study on the ecological importance of wetlands on adjacent DOD property was published in 2004 (Martin et al., 2004). The study revealed that DOD wetlands are vibrant and play a critical role in the maintenance of wildlife, especially migrating and endemic birds. In addition, this study revealed that the exotic saltcedar (*Tamarix chinensis.*) is well established at most wetland sites. This study did not evaluate geologic controls on groundwater flow or potential threats to source water.

The condition and trend of flow in the Lost River is unknown. Anecdotal reports suggest that flow is decreasing. The potential for other geologically similar features on DOD property exists and information on those features could prove useful in evaluating trends for the Lost River. Martin et al. (2004) lists several possibilities, including Brazel Lake, Barrel Spring and Tularosa Creek. Historic aerial photographs may be useful background information for an inventory of wetlands. Aerial photos available online through Google Earth reveal arroyos with vegetation to the north and along the Jarilla Fault. A stream gage would provide useful long-term data and would need to be located on DOD property.

Groundwater

A Master's Thesis from University of Texas at El Paso (Barud-Zubillaga, 2000) reported that annual water levels in observation wells within WHSA did not decline and did not vary by more than 3.9 inches. The report notes that several of the wells do show some response to precipitation and seasonal changes. Recent measurements of water samples from these same wells suggest that groundwater is low in total dissolved solids (Bustos, personal communication, 2008) indicating that recharge to the shallow aquifer may largely be due to precipitation.

More is known about the condition of deeper, regional groundwater resources. Groundwater reports for the surrounding communities indicate that groundwater levels are declining. Along the eastern side of the Tularosa Basin, these declines are limited to areas adjacent to the well fields. However, groundwater declines due to withdrawals by the City of El Paso are projected to propagate north to the monument (El Paso Water Utilities, 2004). Declines in the once flowing Garton well may be due to deterioration of the well casing or an indication that water level declines are more widespread than previously thought.

What are the current or potential threats to the geologic and water resources?

Geologic Resources

Dune Stability - Invasive Plants

Introduced into the United States in the early 1900s as an ornamental shrub, wind break, and shade tree, saltcedar creates vegetative pedestals by transpiring enough groundwater to lower the water table in the immediate area, drying out the surrounding sand, which then erodes away. Interdunal areas are stabilized by high groundwater levels, which dry out the surrounding sand that erodes away. This alone alters dune distribution but the pedestals also change local wind patterns imposing further control on where dunes occur. Continued influence of saltcedar may result in distribution patterns of dunes reflecting occurrence of the invasive species.

Figure 19 shows the approximate locations of areas where saltcedar may occur in the monument. The University of New Mexico is currently producing a more detailed map of saltcedar occurrence (Bustos, personal communication, 2009). Comparing the new distribution map to dune distribution in the monument may highlight areas where saltcedar poses threats to dune resources.

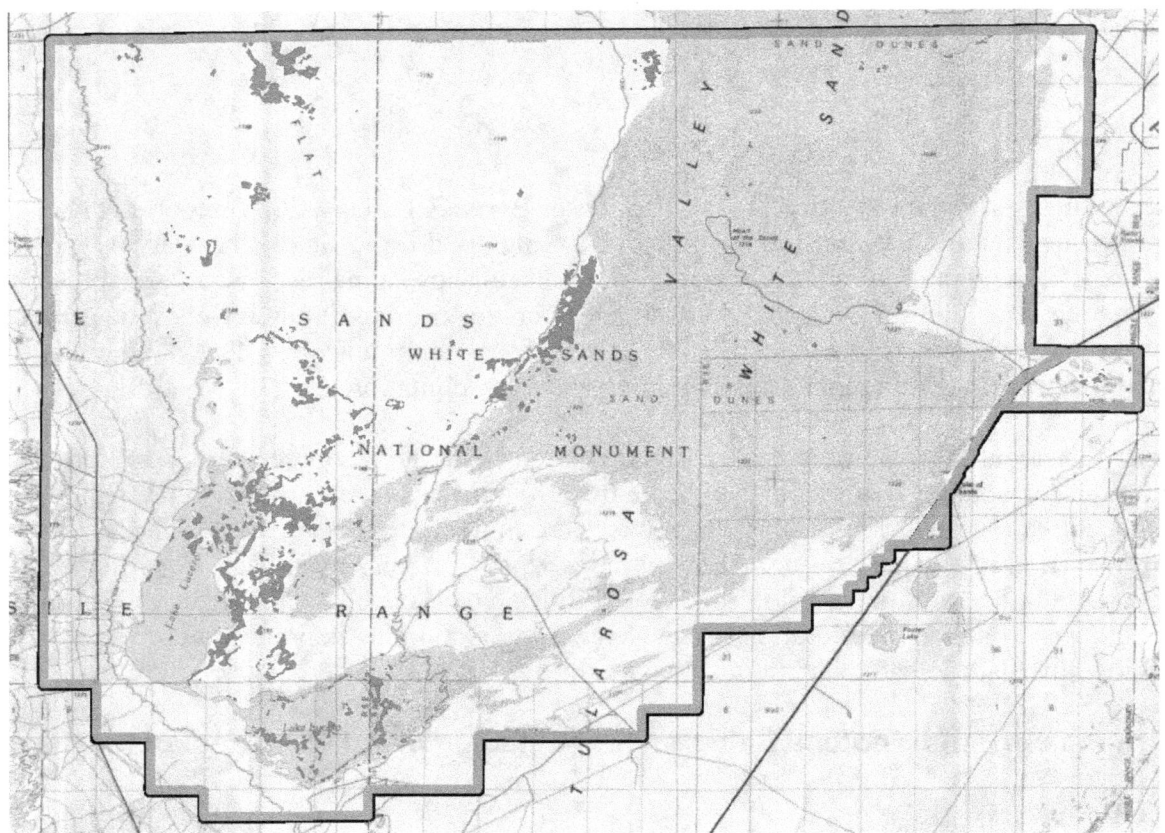

Figure 19. Distribution of saltcedar areas within White Sands National Monument. These areas are shown in purple. (GIS data provided by White Sands National Monument).

Erosion

Erosion is a natural process at WHSA; however man-made structures in certain areas may concentrate the effects of erosion and threaten both natural resources and monument facilities. Road culverts on the west side of the monument concentrate flow and accelerate erosion. This has damaged some cultural resources, specifically the Huntington Site (KellerLynn, 2008). Berms and alterations to channel morphology eliminate the beneficial effects of water on certain portions of the landscape and concentrate it on others, altering vegetation and erosional patterns (Bennett, 2004). Man-made structures such as roads, tanks, buried fiber optic cables, water lines, roads and trails all impact runoff patterns. Increased erosion and the accidental excavation of cultural resources are a real possibility. Periodic flooding can also transport contaminants from DOD property onto WHSA, either by causing a spill or carrying previously spilled hazardous materials into the monument

Dissolution around buried features such as buried water lines and fiber optic cables and trenches has caused the formation of sink holes and other karst-like features. No naturally-occurring karst is documented within the monument (KellerLynn, 2008). Parking lots and buildings are also at risk as rainwater runoff and water from other sources dissolves underlying gypsum layers.

Wind: Erosion or deposition of sand due to wind affects facility development and requires increased maintenance especially along the Loop Road which is often covered by wind-blown sand. Decisions for the location of new facilities should consider sand movement patterns across the monument.

Hillslope Processes: Coalesced alluvial fans on the west side of the monument are known sources of debris flows caused by storm events. These debris flows can transport large boulders onto roads and destroy fences. There are also documented cases of fatalities due to debris flows on the missile range and in a nearby BLM campground (KellerLynn, 2008).

Park staff is concerned about impacts from road building on the west side of the monument. Road structures and culverts concentrate runoff and erode downstream monument natural and cultural resources (KellerLynn, 2003). A full inventory of these structures and assessment of at risk resources has not been done.

Water Resources

Groundwater Mining

The Office of the New Mexico State Engineer, on May 19, 1997, recognized the Tularosa Basin as a mined basin and instituted policies and procedures to allow a specified amount of de-watering during a forty-year planning period. The office specified that water level decline rates should not exceed 2.5 feet per year and the application of water shall not be contrary to the public welfare. Water quality suitable for domestic, municipal, and agriculture and industrial purpose shall be maintained and a major portion of the freshwater saturated thickness shall be reserved for uses beyond the 40-year planning period (New Mexico State Engineer Office, 1997). Municipal use represents the largest draw on freshwater resources in the area and projected water level declines are limited to areas adjacent to well fields used to supply municipal customers.

To date, water resource development has been restricted to the eastern basin. The regional 40-year water development plan states that this trend will continue. Reports indicate that flow in the Lost River has been diminished by consumptive use by the city of Alamogordo and communities in the Sacramento Mountains (KellerLynn, 2003). Agricultural operations may contribute to diminished streamflow as well (Finch, personal communication, 2009). The city of Alamogordo recently extended groundwater withdrawals to brackish water with a proposal to construct a desalinization facility north of the Village of Tularosa. The right to withdraw groundwater is based on permit T-3825 and specifies a diversion of 4000 acre-feet-per-year (AFY) of brackish water to divert 3200 AFY of fresh water. The agreement also states that groundwater rights at other city wells be reduced; the net reduction in all city wells amounts to 61 percent of the new right (New Mexico State Engineer Office, 2007). The pipeline needed to convey this water is currently under environmental review. This agreement will satisfy projected water needs for the City of Alamogordo until 2043 (New Mexico State Engineer Office, 2007). Other consumers of water on the eastern side include agricultural interests. Withdrawals of groundwater for irrigation along the upper portions of the Lost River, in the area west of state highway 54, and north of highway 82, may reduce flow in the Lost River. Applications to the New Mexico Office of the

State Engineer for groundwater pumping rights within the Tularosa Basin need to be carefully monitored by the NPS.

Since the Jarilla Fault acts as a barrier to groundwater movement, it could preclude the propagation of water level declines from the eastern part to the western part of the basin. However, groundwater from the eastern basin may contribute to supplies in the western basin. Likely sources for the groundwater moving from the eastern basin to the western basin are highly transmissive subsurface gravel lenses that are recharged at the eastern basin margin. The Jarilla Fault would force this water to the surface just west of Alamogordo. The nature and timing of dewatering has not been reported and as such, interpreting the causes is difficult. However, highly transmissive gravels would be a likely target for any drilling project. The dewatering of streams entering the dune field could be related to anecdotal reports of wetland decline. A decline in wetlands indicates a declining water table and would represent a threat to dune stability.

The Tularosa Basin is connected to the Hueco Bolson to the south. The Hueco Bolson extends across the state line into Texas and is a primary water source for the city of El Paso. Under the "Rule of Capture", groundwater extraction in Texas is not regulated. A landowner is legally entitled to any water that can be captured from a piece of land, even it that withdrawal drains water from an adjoining piece of property. El Paso has constructed a large desalinization facility to maximize their use of the basin aquifer. Computer modeling of the impacts of groundwater pumping indicate that declining water levels in the Hueco Bolson will propagate north into the Tularosa Basin (El Paso Water Utilities, 2004). Furthermore, each of the Department of Defense facilities has its own water supply. Currently, a comprehensive model that brings together all current and potential use within the basins does not exist. Without such a model it is difficult to predict how declining water levels will propagate and superimpose.

Declining water levels will increase dune mobility and decrease biological activity in interdune areas. The essential question concerns the relationship of the local shallow aquifer to the basin aquifer. The seriousness of this issue is evident in the impact of the invasion of Tamarisk trees in the northeast portion of the monument. Here the exotic tree consumes enough water to lower the water table locally and cause the erosion of the interdune areas.

Groundwater lenses in the monument are discontinuous and have limited areal extent. Because of this they are susceptible to drought and over production. Over production of one of these lenses could result in declining water levels or saline water intrusion.

Water Pollution and Groundwater Contamination

The groundwater resources in the monument include fresh groundwater in the alluvial fans on the western side and abundant saline groundwater. The water table generally lies between 3 and 9 feet below the surface. Potential sources for contamination include over 50 hazardous waste sites on adjacent DOD land, spills on Highway 70, and errant missiles that occasionally land on monument property (Bustos, personal communication, 2008). WHSA is completely surrounded by military facilities involved in the research and development of weapons and weapons delivery systems. Missile craters are a common feature of the landscape and errant missiles represent a direct vector for contamination. Accidental spills of fuel and industrial products during normal operations have the potential to cause localized groundwater contamination. Hazardous waste sites consist of volatile organic compounds (VOC), fuels, polychlorinated biphenyls (PCBs), dioxins, nitrate compounds, heavy metals, radioactive compounds, and pesticides. Groundwater gradients bring groundwater to the monument from the surrounding lands.

Two reported investigations on water contamination were available for this report. In 1998, the USGS analyzed water samples from two wells (MW2 and 3) and the Lost River for contaminants entering the monument from HAFB. Very small concentrations were found but were below detectable limits and below allowable maximum contaminant levels. In 2003, six solid leaf samples from the Lost River were analyzed by the USGS for perchlorate. All samples had concentrations below detectable limits.

The current configuration of monitoring wells may not allow for detection of contaminant plumes from upgradient sources. Better locations would be along the eastern boundary of the monument, with the locations and depths determined by geophysical surveys to identify higher permeability lenses or tongues of sediment which would provide preferential paths for groundwater flow.

Climate Change

All regions of the world show an overall net negative impact of climate change on water resources and freshwater ecosystems. Areas in which runoff is projected to decline are likely to face a reduction in the value of the services provided by water resources. The beneficial impacts of increased annual runoff in other areas are likely to be tempered in some areas by negative effects of increased precipitation variability and seasonal runoff shifts on water supply, water quality and flood risks (Intergovernmental Panel on Climate Change, 2007).

Climate change has the potential to dramatically impact White Sands National Monument, the Tularosa Basin and the arid Southwest (IPCC, 2007) in general. Large permanent changes in regional precipitation, wind averages and temperature pose risks to the ecological and physical systems currently active in the monument. The complex interplay of the dune system, vegetation and groundwater is a product of the hydroclimatic and hydrologic condition of the past 8,000 years. The future condition of WHSA will depend upon several factors including the application of prudent monitoring and planning actions in light of regional growth and development and the subsequent natural system response to the coming hydroclimatic stressors. Since these factors are interdependent, changes in one may lead to feedback adjustments that fundamentally alter the current resources in the monument. Despite the complexity of predicting climate change, many changes can be expected with some confidence and are summarized below (Gleick and Adams, 2000).

- Temperature increases in the Sacramento Mountains will increase the ratio of rain to snow and decrease the length of the snow storage. It is likely that reductions in snowfall and earlier snowmelt and runoff would increase the probability of flooding early in the year and shorten the run-off season.

- Warmer, drier conditions could result in less vegetation to stabilize existing dunes and larger deflation areas; reactivation of dunes could occur with a change in the relative proportion of dune types and sizes.

- Warmer, drier conditions will alter water supply patterns and likely increase the reliance on groundwater as a primary source of domestic, industrial and agricultural water; a drop in the water table could impact dune formation and retention; less runoff available to feed Lake Lucero could create more dunes moving out of the lake beds.

- Research results suggest that drought frequencies in some areas are likely to change. Models project that the occurrence and severity of droughts could increase as a result of decreases in total rainfall, more frequent dry spells, and higher evaporation. Other models suggest with equal confidence that the frequency and severity of droughts in some regions would decrease as a result of increases in total rainfall and less frequent dry spells. In the arid west and southwest, small changes in precipitation and timing will have a greater proportional impact than similar changes in wetter regions.

- Ecologists have high confidence that climate warming will produce a shift in species distributions northward, with extinctions and extirpations of temperate or cold-water species at lower latitudes, and range expansion of warm-water and cool-water species into higher latitudes. Similar patterns can be expected in elevation distributions, with low-elevation species distributions moving upward, and the potential that new low-elevation niches being available to new colonizers, including invasive exotic species.

- Increased atmospheric carbon dioxide will affect the use of water by vegetation, but the net effects of this and other competing influences are complex and difficult to predict. For instance, increasing CO_2 concentrations in some circumstances can reduce the rate of transpiration in certain plants. This in turn would tend to increase runoff since less water is returned directly to the atmosphere by such vegetation, allowing a greater share of precipitation to reach streams or aquifers. On the other hand rising CO_2 concentrations can also increase plant growth, leading to a larger area of transpiring tissue and a corresponding increase in transpiration. Rising carbon dioxide may also alter plant communities locally on the dunes and in the surrounding regions. Plant species important to dune stability may be lost. Changing plant communities in the surrounding mountains could alter rates of aquifer recharge.

- Changing precipitation cycles could impact biological crusts on soils and in turn might impact the nutrient cycling, moisture retention, and erosion resistance capacity of the soils (KellerLynn, 2003). Increased thunderstorm activity could also impact soil surfaces by diminishing soil crusts and increasing erosion.

Climate change research implies that some climate scenarios can yield conditions that might reduce stresses on local or regional ecosystems. However, experience with complex ecosystem dynamics strongly suggests that stressors that drive ecosystems in any direction away from the natural range of variability of conditions under which they developed will have adverse impacts on that system. Ecohydrologic systems can be highly sensitive to hydroclimatic factors, particularly water quantity, water quality, the probability of extreme events, and flow volumes, rates, and timing. Determining the impacts on WHSA will require additional region-specific, and ecosystem-specific, research.

Recognizing the serious implications that global warming and climate variation will have on the economy and the environment, the Governor of New Mexico signed executive order 05-033 (2005) establishing the New Mexico Climate Change Action Council and the New Mexico Climate change Advisory Group (Weeks, 2007).

Stakeholders, Legislation, and Management Policies

National Stakeholders

U.S. Department of Defense, Holloman AFB and White Sands Missile Range. The DOD maintains active flight and research operations in the vicinity of WHSA. Defense department activities are often classified and or dangerous and have prompted strict security on Holloman AFB and Missile Range lands.

U.S. Bureau of Land Management is responsible for much of the land adjacent to DOD property and influences land use for watersheds above WHSA.

U.S. Forest Service manages many of the watersheds in the surrounding highlands.

U.S. Geological Survey conducts desert and planetary research within and around the monument. The USGS New Mexico Water Resources office in Las Cruces also conducts research and monitoring activities in the vicinity.

Mescalero Apache Reservation encompasses approximately 720 square miles northeast of Alamogordo. The reservation is home to about 4,000 people and includes recreational developments designed to attract tourists.

Tribal Historic Preservation Office implements federal and tribal preservation laws as well as advises and works with federal agencies on the management of tribal historic properties.

U.S. Department of Agriculture's Natural Resource Conservation Service and Agricultural Research Service actively promote soil, water and other natural resource conservation both by conducting and funding research and by communicating with local landowners and managers on best conservation practices.

U.S. Environmental Protection Agency has the mission is to protect human health and the environment.

U.S. Fish and Wildlife Service, Southwest Region 2 seeks to conserve, protect and enhance fish, wildlife and plants and their habitats. The FWS administers the San Andres National Wildlife Refuge.

NASA maintains several space flight testing and training facilities in adjacent DOD lands and supports and conducts planetary research in and around WHSA.

State Stakeholders

New Mexico, Office of the State Engineer administers groundwater allocation in the state.

New Mexico, Interstate Stream Commission administers surface water within the state.

State Historic Preservation Office, overseen by the NPS, grants permits for archaeological surveys and excavations, places properties on the State Register of Cultural Properties and makes recommendations for nomination to the National Register of Historic Places, and reviews and approves state income tax credits for rehabilitation and stabilization of registered properties.

New Mexico, Department of Game and Fish aims to provide and maintain an adequate supply of wildlife and fish. The department manages to conserve wildlife and fish for their use as public recreation and food supply.

Regional Stakeholders

City of Alamogordo and other local communities partially rely on the tourist dollars generated by WHSA. These communities also have a stake in regional water rights and development associated with them may have an impact on WHSA ecosystems and subsequent management strategies.

Southwest Environmental Center is and active conservation association in the region and seeks to protect and restore natural ecoscapes in the vicinity of WHSA.

Academic research is conducted in and around the monument by numerous institutions including University of Texas at El Paso (UTEP), New Mexico State University (NMSU), University of New Mexico (UNM), University of Texas at Austin, (UT Austin), New Mexico Tech and Indiana University. The *Lunar and Planetary Institute* supports and conducts much of this research and serves as a repository for data and information resulting from this research.

Park Specific Legislation

1. Legal Description: White Sands National Monument is located in the Tularosa Basin of south central New Mexico, between the Sacramento and San Andres mountains. Its 144,000 acres are 15 miles southwest of Alamogordo, New Mexico in Otero and Don Ana counties. White Sands Missile Range and Holloman Air Force Base completely surround the monument.

2. Under the authority of 16 U.S.C., Section 3, and Title 36, Code of Federal Regulations, Chapter 1, Parts 1-7, a Compendium of Superintendent's Orders is established for White Sands National Monument
(http://www.nps.gov/whsa/parkmgmt/upload/Compendium%20Jan%2026%202007.pdf). Regulations listed in this compendium are requirements in addition to those listed in Parts 1-7 of Title 36 unless otherwise noted. The specific authority for this regulatory procedure is found in Sections 1.5, 1.6 and 1.7 of Title 36. This Compendium will remain in effect until specifically amended or supplemented by the Superintendent.

3. The primary purpose of the monument is to preserve and protect the most impressive portion of the world's largest gypsum desert. A related purpose of the monument is to preserve all cultural and natural resources, historic structures and wildlife. Pertinent legislation is as follows:

January 18, 1933: White Sands National Monument was established by Herbert Hoover, President of the United States of America, with Presidential Proclamation No. 2025 (47 Stat. 2551)
November 28. 1934: Boundaries enlarged by Presidential Proclamation No. 2108 (49 Stat. 3426)
August 29, 1938: Boundaries were modified by Presidential Proclamation No. 2295, eliminating them from all sections now included in the right-of-way for United States Highway Route 70 (53 Stat. 2465)
June 6. 1942: This Act added the former White Sands Recreational Demonstration Project to the monument (56 Stat. 327)
June 27, 1953: Added public lands to the monument. Presidential Proclamation No. 3024 (18 F.R. 3683)
November 10. 1978: This Act adjusted the monument boundaries by adding certain lands and deleting others (92 Stat. 3467)
September 28, 1996: This Act adjusted the monument boundaries by adding certain lands and deleting others (110 Stat. 2803)

Federal Legislation

National Park Service Organic Act of 1916 created the NPS and includes a significant management provision stating that the NPS *shall promote and regulate the use of the federal areas known as national parks, monuments, and reservations by such means and measures as conform to the fundamental purpose of the said parks, monuments, and reservations, which purpose is to conserve the scenery and the natural and historic objects and the wild life therein and to provide for the enjoyment of the same in such manner and by such means as will leave them unimpaired for future generations.* The Organic Act also authorizes the NPS to *regulate the use* of national parks and develop rules, regulations and detailed policies to implement the broad policies provided by Congress. Rules and regulations for the national park system are described in the *Code of Federal Regulations* (Title 36).

General Authorities Act of 1970 strengthened the 1916 *Organic Act*, stating that lands in all NPS units, regardless of title or designation, shall have a common purpose of preservation. All water resources in the national park system, therefore, are equally protected by federal law. It is the primary duty of the NPS to protect those resources unless otherwise indicated by Congress.

Redwood National Park Act of 1978 amended the *General Authorities Act* of 1970, identifying the *high public value and integrity of the national park system* as reason to manage and protect all park system units. The act further stated that no activities should be allowed that will compromise the *values and purposes for which these various areas have been established*, except where specifically authorized by law or provided for by Congress.

National Parks Omnibus Management Act of 1998 outlined a strategy to improve the ability of the NPS to provide high-quality resource management, protection, interpretation, and research in the national park system by:

- Fostering the collection and application of the highest quality science and information to enhance management of units of the national park system;
- Authorizing and initiating cooperative agreements with colleges and universities, including but not limited to land grant schools, along with creating partnerships with other Federal and State agencies, to construct cooperative study units that will coordinate multi-disciplinary research and develop integrated information products on the resources in national park system units and/or the larger region surrounding and including parks;
- Designing and implementing an inventory and monitoring program of national park system resources to collect baseline information and to evaluate long-term trends on resource condition of the national park system, and;
- Executing the necessary actions to fully and properly apply the results of scientific study to park management decisions. Additionally, all NPS actions that may cause a significant adverse effect on a park resource must conduct unit resource studies and administratively record how study results were considered in decision making. The trend in resource condition in the national park system shall be a critical element in evaluating the annual performance of the NPS.

Federal Water Pollution Control Act of 1972, also known as the *Clean Water Act*, strives to restore and maintain the integrity of U.S. waters. The Clean Water Act grants authority to the states to implement water quality protection through best management practices and water quality standards. Section 404 of the act requires that any dredged or fill materials discharged into U.S. waters, including wetlands, must be authorized through a permit issued by the U.S. Army Corps of Engineers, which administers the Section 404 permit program. Additionally, Section 402 of the act requires that pollutants from any point source discharged into U.S. waters must be authorized by a permit obtained from the National Pollutant Discharge Elimination System (NPDES). All discharges and storm water runoff from major industrial and transportation activities, municipalities, and certain construction activities generally must be authorized by permit through the NPDES program. NPDES permitting authority typically is delegated to the state by the U.S. Environmental Protection Agency.

Safe Drinking Water Act (42 USC 3001 et seq.) applies to developed public drinking water supplies. It sets national minimum water quality standards and requires testing of drinking water.

> *2006 NPS Management Policies*: The NPS will determine the quality of park surface and groundwater resources and avoid, whenever possible, the pollution of park waters by human activities occurring within and outside of parks.
>
> - Work with appropriate governmental bodies to obtain the highest possible standards available under the Clean Water Act for the protection of park waters.
> - Take all necessary actions to maintain or restore the quality of surface water and groundwater within the parks consistent with the Clean Water Act and all other applicable federal, state, and local laws and regulations;
> - Enter into agreements with other agencies and governing bodies, as appropriate, to secure their cooperation in maintaining or restoring the quality of park water resources.
>
> *2006 NPS Management Policies:* The NPS will manage watersheds as complete hydrologic systems, and will minimize human disturbance to the natural upland processes that deliver water, sediment, and woody debris to streams. The NPS will achieve the protection of watershed and stream features primarily by avoiding impacts to watershed processes to proceed unimpeded.

Executive Order 11990: Wetlands Protection requires the NPS to 1) exhibit leadership and act to minimize the destruction, loss, or degradation of wetlands; 2) protect and improve wetlands and their natural and beneficial values; and 3) to refrain from direct or indirect assistance of new construction projects in wetlands unless there are no feasible alternative to such construction and the proposed action includes all feasible measures to minimize damage to wetlands.

> *NPS 2006 Management Policies:* The NPS will manage wetlands in compliance with NPS mandates and the requirements of Executive Order 11990 (Wetland Protection), the Clean Water Act, and the Rivers and Harbors Appropriation Act of 1899, and the procedures described in D.O. 77-1. The service will 1) provide leadership and take action to prevent the destruction, loss, and degradation of wetlands; 2) preserve and enhance the natural and beneficial values of wetlands; and 3) avoid direct and indirect support of new construction in wetlands unless there are not practicable alternatives and the proposed action includes all practicable measures to minimize harm to wetlands. The NPS will implement a "no net loss of wetlands" policy.

Executive Order 11988: Floodplain Management has a primary objective *...to avoid to the extent possible the long- and short-term adverse impacts associated with the occupancy and modification of floodplains and to avoid direct and indirect support of floodplain* *development wherever there is a practicable alternative.* For non-recurring actions, the order requires that all proposed facilities must be located outside the boundary of the 100-year floodplain. Barring any feasible alternatives to construction within the floodplain, adverse impacts are to be minimized during the design phase of project planning. NPS guidance for this executive order can be found in D.O. 77-2.

> *2006 NPS Management Policies:* In managing floodplains on park lands, the NPS will 1) manage for the preservation of floodplain values; 2) minimize potentially hazardous conditions associated with flooding; and 3) comply with the NPS Organic Act and all other federal laws and executive orders related to the management of activities in flood-prone areas, including Executive Order 11988 (Floodplain Management), NEPA, applicable provisions of the Clean Water Act, and the Rivers and Harbors Appropriation Act of 1899. Specifically the NPS will:
> - Protect, preserve, and restore the natural resources and functions of floodplains;
> - Avoid the long-and short-term environmental effects associated with the occupancy and modifications of floodplains; and
> - Avoid direct and indirect support of floodplain development and actions that could adversely affect the natural resources and functions of floodplains or increase flood risks.

Clean Air Act of 1970 (as amended in 1990) regulates airborne emissions of a variety of pollutants from area, stationary, and mobile sources. The amendments to the act were added primarily to fill gaps in earlier regulations pertaining to acid rain, ground level ozone, stratospheric ozone depletion and air toxics, and also to identify 189 hazardous air pollutants. The act directs the U.S. Environmental Protection Agency to study these pollutants, identify their sources, determine the need for emissions standards and develop and enforce appropriate regulations.

National Environmental Policy Act of 1969 (NEPA) requires that any action proposed by a federal agency that may have significant environmental impacts shall *utilize a systematic, interdisciplinary approach which will insure the integrated use of the natural and social sciences and the environmental design arts in planning and in decision making which may have an impact on man's environment.*

Endangered Species Act of 1973 requires the NPS to identify all federally listed endangered, threatened and candidate species that occur within each park unit and promote their conservation and recovery. The act requires that any activity funded by federal monies that has the potential to impact endangered biota must be consulted through the Secretary of Interior. It requires agencies to protect designated critical habitats upon which endangered and threatened species depend. Although not required by law, it also is NPS policy to identify, preserve and restore state and locally listed species of concern and their habitats.

Invasive Species (Executive Order 13112): enhances and furthers the existing authority of the federal government to assist in preventing and controlling the spread of invasive species.

Paleontological Resources Preservation Act of 2009 (PRPA), 16 U.S.C. Section 470aaa et seq., directs the Secretaries of the Interior and Agriculture to implement a comprehensive paleontological resource management program on federal lands. The Act's requirements will result in increased protection, enhanced management tools, and greater scientific and public understanding of NPS fossil resources. PRPA requires the agencies to: 1) promulgate regulations as soon as practical; 2) develop plans for fossil inventories, monitoring, and scientific and educational use; 3) manage and protect paleontological resources on Federal land using scientific principles and expertise; 4) establish a program to increase public awareness about the significance of paleontological resources; 5) allow casual collection of common invertebrate and plant fossils on BLM, Forest Service and Bureau of Reclamation lands where consistent with the laws governing those lands; 6) manage fossil collection via specific permitting requirements; 7) curate collected fossils in accordance with the Act's requirements; 8) implement the Act's criminal and civil enforcement, penalty, reward and forfeiture provisions; and 9) protect information about the nature and specific location of fossils where warranted. The Act authorizes appropriations necessary to carry out these requirements.

2006 NPS Management Policies: Geologic Resource Management - the NPS will preserve and protect geologic resources as integral components of park natural systems. As used here, the term "geologic resources" includes both geologic features and geologic processes. The Service will (1) assess the impacts of natural processes and human-related events on geologic resources, (2) maintain and restore the integrity of existing geologic resources, (3) integrate geologic resource management into Service operations and planning, and (4) interpret geologic resources for park visitors (NPS, 2006 §4.8).

2006 NPS Management Policies: Soil Resource Management - the NPS will actively seek to understand and preserve the soil resources of parks, and to prevent, to the extent possible, the unnatural erosion, physical removal, or contamination of the soil, or it's contaminate of other resources. Park will obtain surveys of soils adequate for the management of park resources. All soil surveys will follow National Cooperative Soil Survey Standards. Products will include soil maps, determination of the physical and chemical characteristics of soils, and the interpretations needed to guide resource management and development decisions (NPS, 2006 § 4.8.2.4).

State of New Mexico

Water quality standards relative to WHSA are guided by the Clean Water Act as promulgated by the State of New Mexico (New Mexico Water Quality Control Commission, 2007). Details to these standards were provided earlier in this report.

Restoration plans called Total Maximum Daily Loads (TMDLs) are prepared for impaired waters in New Mexico. The objective of the TMDLs is to restore impacted waters to where they meet their respective state designated uses. Water listed as impaired in

Executive Order 05-033 (2005) established the New Mexico Climate Change Action Council and the New Mexico Climate Change Advisory Group (CCAG). The CCAG shall review and provide recommendations to the Governor's office regarding climate change policy.

Water Rights

New Mexico water law follows the doctrine of prior appropriation. The right to use water is established by placing it to beneficial use and is maintained as long as water use continues. Rights established earlier in time are senior, and must be satisfied before, those rights established later. State law requires a permit for any water use other than small domestic or stock wells or small stock reservoirs. WHSA has water rights to surface diversion and groundwater extraction for the Dog Canyon area.

WHSA had state water rights to surface-water diversion and groundwater extraction for the Dog Canyon area. Since 1956, Holloman Air Force Base has supplied all water needs for the monument. In 1999, these rights were transferred to HAFB who agreed to meet the water supply needs of the monument in perpetuity.

Literature Cited

Allmendinger, R. J., and F. B. Titus, 1973. Regional Hydrology and Evaporative Discharge as a Present-day Source of Gypsum at White Sands National Monument, New Mexico. New Mexico Bureau of Geology Open File 55.

Barud-Zubillaga, A., 2000. A Conceptual Model of the hydrogeology of White Sands National Monument, south-central New Mexico [M.S. Thesis]: University of Texas at El Paso

Bennett, J. 2004. Grasslands not Badlands; grassland restoration and soil conservation in Big Bend National Park. 6th Symposium on the Natural Resources of the Chihuahuan Desert, Chihuahuan Desert Research Institute. Sul Ross State University. Alpine, Texas October 15-16, 2004.

Burns, A. W., and D. L. Hart, Jr., 1988. Simulated water-level declines caused by ground-water withdrawals near Holloman Air Force Base, Otero County, New Mexico: U.S. Geological Survey Water-Resources Investigations Report 86-4324, 44 p.

Bustos, D. 2008/2009. Personal Communication. White Sands National Monument, Chief of Resource Management. Alamogordo, New Mexico.

Chapin, C. E., 1971. The Rio Grande Rift, pt. 1: modifications and additions: New Mexico Geological Society, Guidebook 22, pp. 191-202.

Clemons, R. E., 1996. A trip through space and time, Las Cruces to Cloudcroft: New Mexico Bureau of Mines and Mineral Resources, Scenic Trip 15, 194 p.

Davey, A. D., K. T. Redmond, and D. B. Simeral, 2007. Weather and Climate Inventory National Park Service, National Park Service Natural Resource Technical Report NPS/CHDN/NRTR-2007/034, 87 pp.

El Paso Water Utilities, 2004. Hueco Bolson Groundwater conditions Report, El Paso Area. http://www.epwu.org/water/hueco_bolson.html.

Finch, S. T., 2009. Personal Communication. John Shomaker and Associates, Inc. Water-Resource and Environmental Consultants. Albuquerque, New Mexico.

Finch, S.T., 2006. Predicted drawdown effects and evaluation of potential saline encroachment due to pumping under city of Alamogordo. Permit #'s T-3825 through T-3825-S-9. John Shomaker and Associates, Inc. Water-Resource and Environmental Consultants. Albuquerque, New Mexico.

Fryberger, S. G., 2001. Geological Overview of White Sands National Monument: Southwest Parks and Monuments Association and NPS website, 9 chapters with illustrations. (http://www.nps.gov/archive/whsa/Geology%20of%20White%20Sands/GeoHome.html)

Gleick, P.L., and D. B. Adams, 2000. Water: The Potential Consequences of Climate Variability and Change for the Water Resources of the United States. The Report of the Water Sector Assessment Team of the National Assessment of the Potential Consequences of Climate Variability and Change [For] the U.S. Global Change Research Program.

Guo, Y., J. Zhao, X. Zuo, S. Drake and X. Zhao, 2008. Biological soil crust development and its topsoil properties in the process of dune stabilization, Inner Mongolia, China. Environmental Geology, Volume 54, Number 3/April, 2008

Healy, D. L., R. R. Wahl, and F. E. Currey, 1978. Gravity Survey of the Tularosa Basin and Adjacent Areas, New Mexico: U.S. Geological Survey, Open-file Report 78-309, 56 pp.

Herrick, C. L., 1904. Lake Otero, an Ancient Sal Lake Basin in Southeastern New Mexico: American Geologist, no. September, p. 174-189.

Huff, G. F., 2004. Simulation of Ground-Water Flow in the Basin-Fill Aquifer of the Tularosa Basin, South-Central New Mexico, Predevelopment through 2040, U.S. Geological Survey Scientific Investigations Report 2004-5197, 98 pp.

Huff, G. F., 1996, Analysis of Ground-Water Data for Selected Wells near Holloman Air Force Base, New Mexico, 1950-95, U.S. Geological Survey Water-Resources Investigations Report 96-4116, 37 pp.

Intergovernmental Panel on Climate Change, 2007. Climate Change 2007: Impacts, Adaptation, and Vulnerability. Contribution of Working Group II to the Fourth Assessment Report of the Intergovernmental Panel on Climate Change [Parry, Martin L., Canziani, Osvaldo F., Palutikof, Jean P., van der Linden, Paul J., and Hanson, Clair E. (eds.)]. Cambridge University Press, Cambridge, United Kingdom, 1000 pp.

KellerLynn, 2008. Geologic Resource Evaluation Scoping Summary, White Sands National Monument, National Park Service, Geologic Resources Division, 20 pp.

KellerLynn, 2003. Geoindicators Scoping Report for White Sands National Monument, Strategic Planning Goal Ib4, National Park Service, 85 pp.

King, W. E., and V. M. Harder, 1985. Oil and gas potential of the Tularosa Basin-Otero platform- Salt Basin graben area, New Mexico and Texas.

Kocurek, G., M. Carr, R. Ewing, K. G. Havholm, Y. C. Nagar, and A. K. Singhvi, 2007. White Sands dune field, New Mexico: Age, dune dynamics and recent accumulations. Sedimentary Geology 197 (3–4): 313–331.

Livingston Associates and John Shomaker and Associates, 2002. Tularosa Basin and Salt Basin Regional Water Plan, 2000-2040, South Central Mountain RC&D Council, Inc. www.livingston-associates.com/planningstudies.html.

Love, D., 2008/2009. Personal Communication. New Mexico Bureau of Geology and Mineral Resources. New Mexico Institute of Mining & Technology. Socorro, New Mexico.

Love, D., 2008. Written Communication, August, 2008. New Mexico Bureau of Geology and Mineral Resources. New Mexico Institute of Mining & Technology. Socorro, New Mexico.

Martin, C. O., R. A. Fischer, D. E. Evan, M. P. Guilfoyle, and D. W. Burkett, 2004. Ecological Importance of "Water of the United States" and associated Wetlands to Wildlife at the U. S. Army White Sands Missile Range New Mexico, Environmental laboratory, U. S. Army Engineer Research and Development Center, Vicksburg, Mississippi.

McCauley, J. F., 1973. Mariner 9 Evidence for Wind Erosion in the Equatorial and Mid-Latitude Regions of Mars. Journal of Geophysical Research, vol. 72, p. 4123–4137.

McKee, E. D. (ed.). 1979. A study of global sand seas. Geol. Survey Professional Paper 1052.

Mckee, E. D., and Douglass, J. R., 1971. Growth and Movement of Dunes at White Sands National Monument, New Mexico, U.S. Geological Survey Professional Paper 750-D, p.108-114.

Meinzer, O. E., and R. F. Hare, 1915. Geology and Water Resources of the Tularosa Basin, New Mexico: U.S. Geological Society, Water-Supply paper 343, 317 pp.

National Park Service, 2007, Paleontological Resources Inventory and Monitoring – Chihuahuan Desert Network, TIC#D-500.

National Park Service, 2006, Management Policies. U.S. Department of the Interior. Washington D.C. 168 pp.

National Park Service, 2004. NPS Park Planning Program Standards, August 2004. http://planning.nps.gov/policy.cfm

National Park Service, 1997. Baseline Water Quality Inventory and Analysis, White Sands National Monument, Technical Report,NPS/NRWR.NRTR-97/139, U.S. Department of the Interior, Washington D.C.

Neher, R. E. and O. F. Bailey, 1976. Soil Survey of White Sands Missile Range, New Mexico. U.S.D.A. Soil Conservation Service. 1-64.

New Mexico Geological Society, 2002. Geology of White Sands. Eds. V.W. Lueth, D.A. Giles, S.G. Lucas, B.S. Kues, R. Myers, D.S. Ulmer-Scholle.

New Mexico State Engineer Office, 2007. Settlement Agreement between the New Mexico State Engineer and the City of Alamogordo regarding Permit No. T-3825 et al. http://www.ose.state.nm.us/legal_index.html

New Mexico State Engineer Office, 1997. Tularosa Underground Water Basin Administrative Criteria for the Alamogordo-Tularosa Area. http://www.ose.state.nm.us

Orr, B. R., and R. G. Myers, 1986. Water resources in basin-fill deposits in the Tularosa basin, New Mexico: U.S. Geological Survey, Water Resources Investigations Report 85-4219, 94 p. (for a groundwater model)

Pellant, M., P. Shaver, D. A. Pyle and J. Herrick, 2000. Interpreting Indicators of Rangeland Health, U.S. Bureau of Land Management, Technical Reference 1734-6, 119 pp.

Porter, S. D., R. A. Barker, R. M. Slade, Jr., and G. Longley, 2009. Historical perspective of surface water and groundwater resources in the Chihuahuan Desert Network, National Park Service. Edwards Aquifer Research and Data Center, Texas State University.

Reiser, M. H ., J. P. Ward, Jr., and J. T. Richie, 2008. Chihuahuan Desert Network Vital Signs Monitoring Plan: Draft Phase III. National Park Service, Chihuahuan Desert Network, Las Cruces, New Mexico.

Reid, W. H., and M. H. Reiser, 2006, General Summary on the Climate of Chihuahuan Desert Network Parks and some nearby Protected Lands, Chihuahuan Desert Network, Las Cruces, New Mexico.

Reid, W. H., and H. Reiser, 2005. Chihuahuan Desert Inventory and Monitoring Network, Water Resource Information and Assessment Report, Phase 1.

Rosentreter, R., M. Bowker, and J. Belnap, 2007. A field guide to biological soil crusts of western U.S. drylands. U.S. Government Printing Office, Denver, Colorado.

Schulze-Makuch, D., 2002. Evidence for the discharge of hydrothermal water into Lake Lucero, White Sands National Monument, Southern New Mexico. [In] Geology of White Sands, New Mexico Geological Society. Eds. V. W. Lueth, K. A. Giles, S. G. Lucas, B. S. Kues, R. Myers and D. S. Ulmer-Scholle. Fifty-third Annual Field Conference, October 3-5, 2002. pp 325-329.

Seager, W. R., G. H. Mack, and T. F. Lawton, 1997. Structural kinematics and depositional history of a Laramide uplift-basin pair in southern New Mexico. Geological Society of America Bulletin 109: 1389–1401.

Seager, W. R., J. W. Hawley, F. E. Kottlowski and S.A. Kelley, 1987. Geology of east half of Las Cruces and northeast 1 x 2 sheets, New Mexico: New Mexico Bureau of Mines and Mineral Resources, Geologic Map 57, scale 1: 125,000.

Szynkiewicz, A., Pratt, L. M., Glamoclija, M., Moore, C. H., Singer, E. and Bustos D., 2008. Sulfur Isotopes Signatures in Gypsiferous Sediments of the Tularosa and Estancia Basins as Indicators of sulfate sources and the local Holocene Hydrologic Cycle.

U.S. Geological Survey, 2009. National Hydrography Dataset, Geodatabase. http://nhdgeo.usgs.gov/viewer.htm.

Waltemeyer, Scott D., 2001. Estimates of Mountain-Front Streamflow Available for Potential Recharge to the Tularosa Basin, New Mexico: U.S. Geological Survey, Water Resources Investigations Report 01-4013.

Weeks, D., 2007. Water Resource Foundation Report, Bandelier National Monument. Natural Resource Technical Report NPS/NRPC/WRD/NRTR-2007/060. National Park Service, Fort Collins, Colorado. pp. 53.

Appendix A: CHDN Paleontological Resources Inventory Report – WHSA section

Chihuahuan Desert I&M Network Paleontological Resource Summary—Santucci Kenworthy and Visaggi 2007

WHITE SANDS NATIONAL MONUMENT

White Sands National Monument (WHSA) was established on January 18, 1933 in order to preserve one of the world's largest gypsum sand dune fields. The monument lies at the northern end of the Chihuahuan Desert in the Tularosa Basin of south-central New Mexico. The gypsum dune field encompasses 143,733 acres in south central New Mexico.

BASELINE PALEONTOLOGICAL RESOURCE INVENTORIES

The NPS Geologic Resources Division has not yet completed geologic scoping sessions for White Sands National Monument. No formal paleontological resource inventories have been completed for WHSA and no fossils can be substantiated from within the monument. However paleontological discoveries are documented from an area adjacent to the monument boundary (Conrod, personal communication, 1997). Future paleontological field work may yield other paleontological resources both in and around White Sand National Monument.

Herrick (1900) provides one of the earliest descriptions for the geology of the White Sand of New Mexico. Jicha (1954) and Kiver and Harris (1999) present more recent geologic interpretations of the White Sands. Herrick (1961) produced a geologic map for the White Sands area.

The gypsum dunes have accumulated in a large graben that extends southward to the Texas border and northward to the Malpais basalt flows. The graben is part of a major structural feature known as the Rio Grand Rift. The local graben is referred to as the Tularosa Basin graben and is bounded on the west by the San Andres Mountains and by the Sacramento Mountains on the east (Baldridge and Olsen 1989). The Tularosa Basin graben is 37 miles (60 km) wide. Tularosa Basin is a true bolson, a desert area with internal drainage and no discharge outside of the basin.

The northern part of the White Sands dune field grades into yellowish, wind-deposited, quartz sands. The source of the gypsum has been the subject of some scholarly debate, however, the most likely source of the White Sands gypsum seems to be the local Paleozoic formations (LeMone 1987). During the Paleozoic shallow seas advanced (transgression) and retreated (regression) over the New Mexico area. Thick evaporate deposits were deposited during the Permian including the Yeso Formation which consists of over 500 feet (152 m) of gypsum. The Permian Yeso (Spanish for gypsum) Formation is suggested by LeMone (1987) as the most reasonable source for the gypsum at the monument.

The gypsum sand is primarily medium-grained, ranges from angular to subrounded, and has fair to good sorting (LeMone 1987). A wide variety of dune morphologies are documented at the monument including: dome-shaped, V-shaped, U-shaped, blowout, parabolic, barchan, and transverse dunes. Dune heights and rates of movement are directly related to morphology. The tallest dunes rise to 65 feet (20 m) in some areas. Winds blow almost constantly from the southwest with velocities reaching gusts of 55 mph.

Paleontological Resource Potential

There is a limited potential for the discovery of fossils at White Sands National Monument in the future. Historical reports and recent archaeological and geological surveys suggest the possibility of some fragmentary fossils from within the monument and confirmed paleontological resources from outside park boundaries. These fossil-bearing deposits include vertebrate trace fossils from a locality which should be periodically monitored for preservation of paleontological resources.

Vandiver (1936) reports on the possible occurrence of fossil bones and teeth of a mammoth from within the boundaries of the monument. He personally visited the locality referenced for the mammoth remains and was able to find only fragmentary bones. Vandiver (1936) also describes some external molds of plants at WHSA. These appear to be the remains of cacti and other plants which have become replaced or encrusted by gypsum crystals.

Bill Conrod (personal communication, 1997) reports the presence of Pleistocene mammalian trackways on the nearby White Sands Missile Range managed by the Department of Defense. A site visit to a fossil track locality on the White Sands Missile Range, referred to as the "Big Footprints" locality, on September 11, 1981. Geologists John Hawley, David Love (USGS) and Donald Wolberg participated in this site visit. The field party encountered three different types of vertebrate tracks which were preserved as pedestals above the ground surface. The tracks were determined to be mammalian in morphology and likely ascribed to camel, proboscidian, and some other undetermined mammalian track maker.

REFERENCES CITED

Baldridge, W.S. and K.H. Olsen. 1989. The Rio Grande Rife. American Scientist 77: 240-247.

Herrick, C.L. 1900. The geology of the White Sands of New Mexico. Journal of Geology, vol. 8, p. 112-128.

Herrick, E.H. 1961. Geologic map of White Sands Missile Range Headquarters area, Dona Ana County, New Mexico, showing location of wells, contours on the water table, and location of proposed dams, reservoirs and recharge-discharge wells. U.S. Geological Survey, Hydrologic Investigations Atlas.

Jicha, H.L. 1954. The White Sands, a short review. New Mexico Geological Society Guidebook, 5th Field Conference, p. 88-92.

Kiver, E.P. and D.V. Harris. 1999. Geology of U.S. Parklands. John Wiley & Sons, Inc., New York, 902 pp.

LeMone, D.V. 1987. White Sands National Monument, New Mexico. Geological Society of America Centennial Field Guide, Rocky Mountain Section. P. 451-454.

Vandiver, V.W. 1936. Geological Report on White Sands National Monument. Southwestern Monuments Special Report No. 5. Department of Interior, National Park Service, p. 381-400.

ADDITIONAL REFERENCES

Blair, T.C., J.S. Clark, and S.G. Wells. 1990. Quaternary continental stratigraphy, landscape evolution, and application to archeology: Jarilla piedmont and Tularosa graben floor, White Sands Missile Range, New Mexico. Geological Society of America Bulletin 102: 749-759.

Botkin, C.W. 1933. White Sands National Monument. Pam American Geologist, 60: 304-305.

Brady, F.W. 1905. The White Sands of New Mexico: Formation of nearly pure gypsum sand. Mines and Minerals Publication, p. 529-530.

Gould, C.N. 1939. The Great White Sands [of New Mexico]. Mines Magazine, vol. 29, p. 379-381.

Jones, B.R. 1959. A sedimentary study of dune sands, Lamb and Bailey counties, Texas and White Sands National Monument, New Mexico. Master's Thesis, Texas Tech University, Lubbock, Texas, 95 pp. McKee, E.D. 1966. Structure of dunes at White Sands National Monument, New Mexico. Sedimentology, vol. 7 69 pp.

McKee, E.D. and R.J. Moiola. 1975. Geometry and growth of White Sand dune field, New Mexico. Journal of Research U.S. Geological Survey, 3: 59-66.

McKee, E.D. and J.R. Douglass. 1971. Growth and movement of dunes at White Sands National Monument, New Mexico. U.S. Geological Survey Professional Paper, D108-D114.

Russell, C.P. 1935. The White Sands of Alamogordo. National Geographic Magazine, vol. 64, no. 2.

Simpson, E.L. and D.B. Loope. 1985. Amalgamated interdune deposits, White Sands, New Mexico. Journal of Sedimentary Petrology. Vol. 55, p. 361-365.

Talmadge, S.B. 1933. Source and growth of the White Sands of New Mexico. Pan American Geologist, 60: 304.

Weir, J.E. 1965. Geology and availability of groundwater in the northern part of the White Sands Missile Range and vicinity, New Mexico. U.S. Geological Survey Water Supply Paper, 78pp.

DATA SETS DS-WHSA-XXX	White Sands National Monument Paleontological Archives. 5/1985–present. (hard copy data; reports; electronic data; photographs; maps; publications). Originated by Santucci, Vincent; status: Active.
DS-WHSA-XXX	White Sands National Monument Museum Collections. 1/1933–present. (museum specimens, collection records, specimen notes, ANCS+ records). Originated by WHSAstaff; status: Active.

NPS 142/100371, November 2009